Beyond the Team

Also by this author

Team Roles at Work
Management Teams: why they succeed or fail
The Coming Shape of Organization
Changing the Way We Work

CD-ROM

How to Build Successful Teams . . . The Belbin Way

Beyond the Team

R. Meredith Belbin

ELSEVIER
BUTTERWORTH
HEINEMANN

AMSTERDAM • BOSTON • HEIDELBERG • LONDON • NEW YORK • OXFORD
PARIS • SAN DIEGO • SAN FRANCISCO • SINGAPORE • SYDNEY • TOKYO

Elsevier Butterworth-Heinemann
Linacre House, Jordan Hill, Oxford OX2 8DP
30 Corporate Drive, Burlington, MA 01803

First published 2000
Reprinted 2000, 2004, 2005

British Library Cataloguing in Publication Data
Belbin, Meredith
  Beyond the team
  1. Teams in the workplace
  I. Title
  658.4'02

ISBN 0 7506 4641 1

Composition by Genesis Typesetting, Laser Quay, Rochester, Kent
Printed and bound in Great Britain by MPG Books Ltd, Bodmin, Cornwall

Contents

Figures

Preface

Nothing is more rewarding than success, nor as fleeting; nothing is more intriguing than failure, nor as thought-provoking. When a student of Classics at Cambridge I would often ponder on the achievements of the Roman Republic during the century before the birth of Christ, or the glory that was Greece, embodied by Ancient Athens, as the cradle of democracy. From a combination of these two Classical periods stemmed enduring concepts of law and organization, literature and art, pedagogy and medical ethics and the role of sporting events, like the Olympics, in deflecting conflict and turning it into peaceful competition between different peoples and races.

But then it all fell apart. Democracy gave way to tyranny, peaceful trade and co-operation to war and conquest, consultation and learning to brutality and persecution. If a winning formula provides the good life for a limited period, how can it be that all this changes? People do not wittingly throw away what they value. Somehow destabilizing forces enter to destroy what has previously been stable and flourishing. What could those forces be?

Years of study have led me to the belief that two prime causes account for this degeneration. The first, and perhaps the most important, is size change. Communal success can flourish only within certain size limits. Beyond that, waxing size changes character. Unconstrained expansion destroys resources and lays waste the environment. It is notable how many centres of culture and civilization in the ancient world were located in small city-states, exemplified by those fringing the Ionian Sea, such as famed Miletus; by Venice and the cities of medieval Italy; by the Hanseatic cities of the Baltic, and the Flemish cities which gave birth to so many of the world's greatest painters. Their accomplishments occupied a particular time slot in History. Then decline began once these cradles of civilization became engulfed by larger empires and the conditions for enterprise, creativity and freedom of thought were eroded. The small became incorporated into the big, upsetting internal balance and reducing external effectiveness. Bigness, unchecked by insight, corrodes the vitality and creative flair of the small community and team through a variety of insidious pressures, through a panoply of controlling mechanisms or through naked oppression.

Yet there is a further factor that imperils the creative team and the thriving community. That factor lies in becoming isolated; in the failure of the smaller unit to be aware of and to adapt to the wider world. As I write, we are about to enter the New Millennium. Arguably, this might be no more than an arbitrary moment in a time continuum. I incline to think otherwise; that it marks a truly significant turning-point in human history, coinciding with a new era where the world wakens and begins to look outwards, for only recently has the world been likened to a global village with its business conducted in a truly global market.

Several forces have combined to bring this about. On the political front, there is the desire to replace the concept of warring nations with that of a unified world. On the commercial front, there has been the General Agreement on Trade and Tariffs and its successor, the World Trade Organization, both active in lowering the barriers of protectionism. On the financial front, a growing number of nations are keen to remove the uncertainties created by multiple currencies and the crises that stem from the volatility of exchange rates. The launch of the Euro, coinciding with the New Millennium, is bound to be a landmark in facilitating international trade. So the cumulative effect of all these combined developments is to bring about a rising set of challenges that will penetrate into all aspects of working life.

The gain is that there will be greater opportunities for those who are successful in producing goods and services that satisfy wide demands. But there is a downside potentially attached to this new era. Pain awaits those organizations that cannot modify their own rigid rules and structures, where these impede working effectiveness. That is what has prompted the need to look at the basic building blocks of collective and competitive endeavour. In the last analysis, these have their roots in the design of the *job* – the outcome of a *social* process whereby work is assigned, modified and developed in particular patterns.

Jobs occur at every level and at every size of organization. Yet my contention is that no satisfactory, easily comprehended, and universal language has existed for communicating the nature of this aggregation of working activities. With this in mind I first set out some ideas in my earlier book *Changing the Way We Work*. A new colour-based system was introduced and proved easy to comprehend and apply, being especially useful in overcoming the verbal language impediments that beset the organization of any international workforce. In the further interests of a wider dissemination, we sponsored an introductory film, *Does the Team Work?* made in conjunction with Video Arts. The film briefly sets out the basics of the system and takes place on a manned rocket on its journey to Mars. Mission Control's bureaucratic approach to jobs has disempowered the team, now bereft of the initiative to handle its own problems. The team was aware of its team roles but not of its *work roles*. And so a new language came into being. Only after an intergalactic consultant dropped in to advise on the problem did the journey to Mars proceed on a satisfactory course.

The first successful trials of work roles, and its associated systems, have taken place not of course in space but actually in the UK and Sweden, while a number of parallel projects are currently underway in other countries. Team roles and work roles need to operate in close unison if the best effects are to be achieved. While it had originally been my intention to include some case studies in this book, I concluded that this might be premature. Success is so often fleeting, since one component of a newly introduced system tends to create an imbalance in its relations to other parts. Forces that lie outside the team exert a power that a small team can seldom resist. The strongest of those forces external to the team comes from the bigger group in which the team is encased.

I will argue that the differences in behaviour and expectations stem from a conflict in size-cultures. The larger body will be dominated by its own particular set of norms and I hold that there is a world of difference between the psychology of the team and the psychology of the group. Large groups look for unifying notions; they produce leaders, structures and regulations and using that power impose their will on those below. And when that occurs, groups ultimately swallow teams. Yet the irony, in my view, is that teams are more efficient than groups.

So is there a solution? I have postulated within this book that a genetic factor distorts large group behaviour and its narrowness limits achievement. Such a genetic force might be taken as irresistible. But humans are capable of modifying their behaviour in the light of education and experience. And times are changing. Information technology, opening the door to networking, is exerting a subtle and reforming influence on human organization. A precedent, and a model, is here set by the sophisticated organizational networks of the social insects. I have examined where this trend may lead us in the New Millennium.

The chapters contained in the book are intended to bring out the interconnections between the various parts of a broad approach and are presented as a set of essays that can be read separately, if preferred. The accompanying illustrations are mainly reproductions of OHPs presented at lectures and workshops and for which I have had many requests. Here I hold it is far better that they should be incorporated in a book, with its accompanying text, than that they should stand alone, for no illustrations can hope to be entirely self-explanatory. The visual and the written word acting in mutual support now mark my current position after half a century of continuous work in industry.

Every attempted step forward needs to take account of the foundations others have laid. Some writings have been a source of inspiration and have played a significant part in helping me to formulate my own thoughts. Notable authors who have influenced me in the context of this book include William Bridges, Peter Drucker, Irving Janis, Tony Jay, Eugene Marais, Peter Senge, Riccardo Semler, Edward O. Wilson; and, finally, the late C. Northcote Parkinson, the great uncoverer of what will be described in this book as Pink Work. Much has also been gained from talking to participants at conferences – often those I had not encountered before nor met since. More specifically, I want to thank a number of close colleagues who have helped with advice or preparation of this book, including Ron Johnson and Dawie Gouws and I am grateful to Terri Hunter for allowing me an early look at her much praised doctoral dissertation. I am indebted to Michael Kremer for helping me with some of the more taxing problems posed by the text. Within Belbin Associates, I am grateful to Liz Godfrey for organizing me, to Tom Robson for fruitful discussion and to Peter Lancaster for his help and ideas with illustrations. Finally, I am indebted to Barrie Watson for his ever-positive contribution to developments and the generous use of his time in travelling far and wide in starting up new projects and spreading the message.

I count my blessings as the beneficiary of teamwork and the recipient of wisdom conferred by unseen scholars delving into the accumulated benefits of recorded history. All those to whom my gratitude is expressed in spirit share in any credit and are exonerated from any deficiencies the reader may spot in reading *Beyond the Team*.

R. Meredith Belbin

Introduction

In my first book on the subject of teams I looked at their internal workings. Here I made a distinction between team roles and functional roles. Team roles described a pattern of behaviour that characterizes one person's behaviour in relationship to another in facilitating the progress of a team. Functional roles referred to the role of an employee in terms of the job's technical demands and the experience and knowledge that it requires. Most people when they enter a job start on the basis of the functional demands and only learn about the importance of team roles later. There has certainly been widespread interest in team roles, but very few people ever talk about the functional roles. One day I began to wonder why this should be so.

Roles themselves are enormously important for understanding people in the work situation or in society itself as they create the patterns of behaviour that give shape to the wider social picture. Team roles are valued because they contribute to the effectiveness of the team. But the absence of discussion or interest in functional roles seems strangely out of line with the fact that the route into an appointment nearly always lies through a person's acceptability for a functional role. The functional role is what is implied by the job title. But what does that really mean? A functional role is evidently too broad a term to lend itself to everyday use, for arguably the term is no more than an abstraction of an amalgam. That is to say, it will embrace a professional role, where that is relevant, but it will also embrace rather more than that: it will have to cover all the work that needs to be done, or at least all the important bits.

Observation of the way in which new appointments are absorbed into the organization suggested some regularity in the sequence of events. At the outset professional roles enjoy a dominant position, with the overriding emphasis on qualifications and past experience. The employer says in effect: 'You are well qualified in this area, so I will leave you to it and I am sure you will make something of the job.' In other words, the employer is so favourably impressed with what the applicant can bring to the job that further briefing and instruction is deemed unnecessary. Professional engineers, accountants, lawyers and medical personnel commonly come into this category. In these cases, how to manage the job is taken for granted. Such job induction as exists is confined to introducing the newcomer to colleagues, to basic procedures and to conditions at the workplace.

Most jobs are drawn up with reference points that are largely internal, both to the skills of the jobholder and to the way in which jobs are structured in relation to one another within the organization. In the case of many professional appointments there is a misguided presumption that the appointee knows how to carry out the job without reference to context and without the need for much further guidance. Yet no person at work is an island. There will be interfaces with other people who are sure to present problems. Long-established employees will have closely guarded work territories, which they will defend against any supposed intrusion by the unwary newcomer. And it is common practice for the professional to be expected to join with colleagues from other backgrounds when some important issues come to the fore. That is why an understanding of team roles plays such an important part in enabling professionals to adjust to their jobs and each other. Yet a belief persists that the professional can create a job without assistance. It may happen in some cases but more often it leads to a crisis of misunderstanding. Take the typical case of a computer expert appointed to a company lacking in computer expertise in the hope that the appointment will lead to more advanced practices. The newcomer will ask: 'What is it that you want me to do?' Only to receive the reply: 'I thought a professional would know what the job needs and that you were going to tell us.' In industry a clear-cut hierarchy allows such issues to be raised. In the medical field, in contrast, many highly qualified people move in their own orbit and have near absolute control over their own operations. There may be expectations that they will consult with others, but should they prefer to keep their own counsel, that position cannot easily be changed by outside intervention.

Appointing professionals to a job presents its own set of problems. Behaviour within the job is not open to easy manipulation. A very different situation presents itself when less specialized appointments are made. Here the emphasis swings in the other direction. The job will be precast by the employer; it will be offered as on a plate at interview, so that what the job allows and demands set the scene for occupational behaviour. Now the emphasis shifts from the professional role to whatever roles the work may require. The difficulty here is that in spite of much paperwork directed to this end, there has been no disciplined method for communicating work roles that is clear and unambiguous and acceptable to both parties engaged in the process. As things stand at present, the behaviour required by the job will have to be extracted and interpreted by the prospective employee from what may often seem a jumbled mass of words.

If an overview is now taken of how any job is to be interpreted by the jobholder, we see that every job may encompass three possible roles. There is the professional role, the team role and the work role. Any job may be approached from each of these angles. Whichever approach is selected has a big bearing on what the job produces. Problems are liable to arise if jobs are viewed from a single standpoint to the detriment of the other two aspects. The risk is a loss of perspective in the way in which the job is conducted. Every person who enters a new job should consider his or her position from the point of view of these three forces. Equally, every manager who makes an appointment may usefully conduct an interview with a view to eliciting which of these three forces is going to exert the strongest effect on an appointee's behaviour.

As a general rule it is fair to assume that, apart from social and recreational activity, all human groups engage in some form of work for which meaningful roles need to be created and sustained. That fundamental principle holds good for organizations large and small. To understand how jobs are best created and work distributed in organizations of varying sizes forms the central theme of this book. The three roles that I have used as the basis for understanding work behaviour, and for channelling it in the required direction, are meaningful in everyday language and so can be employed in a general sense. But I think it important that they should also acquire a specific meaning. Otherwise the terms may slide and be used loosely and eventually fail to make the distinctions required. Here it is easy to establish the point with *team roles*, for I have studied and written about this area for quite some time. The roles, which are nine in number, have acquired a technical meaning that is widely understood and embody certain essential concepts. I have restated what we know about them in Chapter 1 so that the reader will know that the term *team role* is being used in a precise sense without the need to cast it in italics. Even so, I have thought fit in Chapters 2 and 3 to focus on the meaning of *team* to offset the risk of that term becoming corrupted. The problem arises because *teamwork* has become a fashionable buzzword – one commonly applied to any group that needs to be presented in a favourable light. Hence, before returning to roles, I have taken a strong line on differentiating between teams and groups, for it is my contention that the psychology of teams and groups embrace quite different principles.

That risk of corruption does not occur in the case of the term *work role* for, as far as I am aware, it is not in common usage. That allows me to speak of work roles in Chapter 4 and thereafter in a well-defined sense without italics and without any risk of confusion. By employing the concept of team roles and work roles in conjunction with one another, with the now widely used software *Interplace* supporting the former and the newly introduced software *WorkSet* supporting the latter, great strides have been made in re-establishing a new equilibrium between people and work. This venture has brought with it a variety of experiences that has caused us to look again at many standard practices. Chapters 5 to 11 reflect our experiences that have spelt out the need for many reforms. What becomes ever more apparent is that one cannot change one part of a system without affecting other parts. That demands a large systems change if real forward steps are to be undertaken. So the middle sections of this book deal with changes that are desirable, which we have brought about in some cases, and for which we have seen real evidence of benefits. Yet those changes are very difficult to establish on any scale conflicting as they do with the compulsions of a larger body. Decisions made at the apex of a hierarchy and imposed on the team are liable to block its vitality and enterprise. Few teams can resist these pressures. The exception arises only when a mature team believes in what it is doing, is convinced of its efficacy and can cultivate a *political* role in its dealings with the wider group. A mature team basks in its inner strength and by outward action can defend and, if need be, revise its own terms of reference.

Such revisions can only be taken so far. In the final chapters of this book I have looked at the problems of the *mega-group*. Ultimately, groups may become so large that they cannot be assembled at any one time and place. The nation state may comprise peoples of varied ethnic origins with different mother tongues and historical traditions. Then the focus of roles shifts from individuals to institutions. What makes the nation state a living organism depends on how well and coherently its *work* is distributed.

Here there is much to be learned about how work can be managed from what already exists in nature. Hence I have tried to extract lessons from the natural world. In evolutionary terms our large-scale human societies are of relatively recent origin, having grown out of small roving bands of hunters and gatherers. So it is understandable that we compare unfavourably in some respects with species that are better equipped by their genetic inheritance for a communal existence. The driving mechanism of evolution has been the combination of variation with the survival of the fittest. Competitive advantage always emerges as the long-term winner. It is almost certain that if better forms of social organization and work behaviour can meet the needs of human populations denser than those which have long populated planet Earth, those models will eventually be discovered. My belief is that it is time to look beyond our current understanding of teams and to realize in tackling the wider problems that confront us still, the social insects have got there first. In this new age of networking, their message for us has a timely relevance. We should have the humility to give closer examination to their proven formulae for effectiveness in a belief that a few well-chosen strategies may improve the format of human society. Against that background there is a case for experimentation, for that is the only sure road to progress.

Chapter

1

The impact of team roles

Small human units can often work conspicuously well. Here it seems a positive sign that surveys of managerial opinion indicate that teamwork is foremost among the matters that will demand attention from management in future years. It is already becoming plain that people in business and in the public services are spending more and more of their time locked in discussions and in meetings. Given this situation, the clear need is to make teamwork and other group activity more effective.

This subject has received due attention from my previous books – *Management Teams: Why They Succeed or Fail* and the later *Team Roles at Work*. It has also gained the attention of a number of other writers including, and notably, Katzenbatch in *The Wisdom of Teams*. Teamwork should supposedly cover the components of the composite word – teams and work. In practice, however, the literature has focused more on the teams than on the work. Here I must plead guilty myself.

This present book attempts to remedy this shortcoming by shifting the focus on to the work to be performed. How is that work communicated? How does the nature of the work affect the social arrangements that are made for its execution?

1

In a very small team, or more especially when two people are working closely together, the focus falls more on the individuals and their working relationships than on the work itself, for effectiveness in performing the work is closely related to how they get on with one another. That is the simple position. And the simple position may serve as a good starting-point. It seems sensible therefore to begin where I left off at an earlier stage in my studies and to present, as concisely as possible, a resumé on the principal findings concerning the forces that affect how teams function.

The fundamentals of team roles emerged after a long period of research. No theory of team roles of which I am aware had been in existence before the outcome of the experimentation at Henley Management College, conducted in conjunction with the Industrial Training Research Unit at Cambridge. The original purpose of that experimentation was practical rather than theoretical. Urgent questions were being posed. How was it that some teams composed on supposedly similar lines, and given the same brief, performed so much better than others? An answer was seen as likely to help the College put together syndicates that would make the best use of their learning opportunities.

The experimental situation made provision for members of syndicates to take a battery of psychometric tests. On the basis of these person-inputs various combinations of people were tried out in companies constructed to compete in a management game. The outputs of their collective endeavours could be represented in financial terms. Hence one company could be fairly described in its operations as more effective than another. The reasons for the relative success or failure of companies were elucidated by the appointment of trained observers. A recording system operated by the observers allowed the contributions that each member made to be measured both in terms of the particular category to which it belonged and in terms of the number of contributions that fell into each category. The observers also added a qualitative report, which allowed them to comment on what they saw as the most important factors underlying the performance of the team.

The collection and analysis of this material eventually allowed a number of hypotheses to be developed. These eventually became predictors. The rank order of finishing between the companies on the basis of their financial performance was forecast on the Monday, when the exercise started, and as soon as the identity of the chairman elected by the team was known, put into a sealed envelope and delivered into the custody of the secretary of the exercise. The envelope was then opened on the Friday, when the exercise concluded, and the result compared with the forecast.

The fact that a forecast could be offered with some measure of success bore testimony to the progress made in grasping the nature of the processes underlying effective teamwork. The main basis of these forecasts lay in the pattern of contributions found to characterize the dynamics of a team and which could be estimated if enough was known about the individuals themselves. There are only a limited number of ways in which people can usefully contribute in executive teamwork; that is what the research revealed. And the essential contributions comprised: co-ordinating the team's efforts, imparting drive, creating ideas, exploring resources, evaluating options, organizing the work, following up on detail, supporting others and providing expertise. The eventual names given to these types of contributor were: Co-ordinator, Shaper, Plant, Resource investigator, Monitor evaluator, Implementer, Completer/finisher, Teamworker and Specialist. Hence each team member could be described in terms of team-role contribution pattern. Individuals varied greatly in their patterns. What was observed, however, was that individuals who were outstanding in one role were often weak in another. That was why the issue of who was combining with whom was a matter of such central importance. Complementary combinations of people proved to be far more effective in their working performance than people with similar profiles competing with each other.

The theory of team roles now began to form an essential part of management education and was employed to good effect in industry, especially in the formation and management of R&D teams, in project teams and management teams generally. However, several academics published studies that showed misgivings on the theory or the methods that were used to delineate team roles or both. Later, however, Terri Hunter of the Department of Psychology in the University of Strathclyde carried out an extensive study into the validity and reliability of team-role theory. She writes:

The team roles and the model were validated through video observation of behaviour using real working teams from a variety of organizations throughout the UK. The teams performed a business game which was video taped. The videos of individuals performing were rated using a checklist of behaviours derived from Belbin's own descriptions of the behaviours and characteristics of the various team roles. Each individual within the team completed two well-established personality measures, namely the OPQ and the 16PF5, from which their team roles were derived. From each of these three measures it was possible to derive three separate team-role profiles for each individual. The team roles derived from both questionnaires had strong relationships with individuals' observed behaviour.

Hunter also looked into an important issue in team-role theory. She found good support for the hypothesis that the more team roles a team has within its members (i.e. a more balanced team), the more successful a team will become (see Hunter, T.A., *Belbin's Team Roles and Model: A Behavioural Validation using the OPQ and 16PF5 Personality Questionnaires* an unpublished PhD thesis, 1999, awaiting publication).

Even without that further academic support, the basic lessons of effective teamwork had taken root. Hunter found from a study of the top 109 trainers in the UK that 'the majority of trainers believed the Belbin concepts to be of practical utility with over half reporting them as the only team-role model used in their organization'. My own book *Management Teams: Why They Succeed or Fail*, containing a self-reporting inventory, no doubt contributed to the rapid spread of the ideas. Self-reporting inventories were becoming very popular in training courses. However, they did suffer from the drawback of being circular in nature. People inevitably agreed with outputs that tallied with their own inputs. An overreliance on self-reporting, as the sole measure of an individual's team role, began to expose a number of problems. While in many cases the self-image accords with how that person is perceived by others, in other cases considerable discrepancies arise. The significance of these discrepancies had not been recognized hitherto. Here was a field that invited strategies for personal adjustment. But before those adjustments could be made, a number of technical steps needed to be taken. This took the form of developing a method for eliciting observer assessments. These assessments could then be related to the data generated by self-reporting and the degree of correspondence between the two could be measured. At that stage it became plain that a manual processing of the data obtained from traditional paper and pencil tests could no longer meet the needs of the situation. Computerization of the various inputs allowed a larger body of information to be handled and the necessary calculations made.

A new line of enquiry now became possible. Investigation at the workplace into individuals identified as being above average in personal effectiveness showed that good correlation between the self and observer perceptions proved positive pointers. On the other hand, where the two sets of information diverged, the misfit became associated with – well, the very same word, misfits in practice, or in other words people whose personal effectiveness was lower than average. Expressed in everyday terms, it meant that most individuals who projected themselves as they really were had advantages in their social and working relationships over those who either preferred to keep themselves hidden or who nurtured illusions about themselves. ('I think I am creative' – ' I don't think he is in the least creative').

Discrepancies, however, were not always a sign of a basic weakness but sometimes of a poor personal strategy in making the most of one's personal strengths. Not infrequently there were examples of individuals who were known to possess a strong track record in an area that was in accord with the self-perception, yet that perception was not shared by their less intimate work associates. Here the problem usually lay in the failure of a person to project the self accurately. Some very modest individuals fell especially into this category. They made few claims about themselves and so were not understood. So without being difficult people they could prove difficult to work with.

All these instances gave support to the recommendation that it was a real advantage to learn about how the self was perceived by others in team-role terms. An adjustment could then be made if the two images were moving too far apart. The learning created a focus: it was to strive to present to others a coherent message by appropriately managing one's words and behaviour.

Another important learning point lay in finding a strategy for adjusting to difficult situations. If someone in a leading position occupies a team role that is best suited to another, is it a good idea to compete? Clearly not, if the lessons from effective and less effective teams are to be taken to heart. Instead those acquainted with team-role theory were encouraged to make team-role sacrifices. They would switch into a less preferred role. Such a move would require conscious self-discipline and in the short-term would bear fruit. And yet it could never operate well for long. Once such a switch became protracted, or the going got tough, strain would show. Preferred behaviour would eventually surface or evident stress would be the price paid for team-role sacrifice.

The messages about team-role theory began to spread and an increasing number of people testified to its value in practice. Eventually the position was reached when we thought any further major development unlikely. Then something strange happened which, on the face of it, seemed paradoxical. As the theory became consolidated and won wide acceptance, predictions in *experimental* situations began to lose their former sharpness.

We began to wonder whether the earlier successful forecasts might have come about by chance, even though statistical analysis of our results rendered that unlikely. Then light on this phenomenon began to emerge. Companies formed experimentally for the purposes of management exercises were observed to differ greatly among themselves in terms of how far they responded to the theory and how they reacted to personal material now available to them. Some of these experimental companies largely ignored the material and pressed on with the exercise, believing that their time would be better spent on the tasks immediately before them. In contrast, other companies took heed of the information available, even if they occasionally took a pessimistic view of their chances. Yet whatever view they took, the readiness of these experimental companies to adjust their behaviour in the light of information about the shape of their team was found to have a positive bearing on their success rate.

The lesson that could be drawn is that *human behaviour operates on a probabilistic not on a deterministic model*. People are not bound to behave in any particular way, since they have the freedom of will to make their own decisions and to react differently. They will exercise that freedom when they have information that helps them. The theory of team roles became in effect a philosophy but one fashioned in the interests of facilitating the way humans work together.

Chapter

2

The team concept under pressure

The momentum for progress towards better teamwork soon began to generate a problem based on its own success. It happened once the word 'teamwork' became accepted in the wider domain of business and public service. The very word embodied and ultimately served to promote the virtues of consultation and co-operation. Such an achievement could be considered a triumph, for its arrival signified a major change in the culture of organizations. Yet in so many triumphs, the seeds of disasters are often embedded within them – and so it was. As soon as it reached a peak, the word teamwork became an invitation to all and sundry to shelter under its mantle. To proclaim a belief in teamwork became a safe way for those in middle management and in personnel functions to gain general approval.

That combination of the exemplary and the warning sign were contained in one experience notable for its varied implications. At a time when interest in teamwork was at its height, I was asked, along with three others, to act in a national competition, sponsored by Rank Xerox, to judge the best team in the public sector. There were many entries and every entry had to be read and assessed by every judge. Eventually four finalists were chosen. There then followed a meeting at Kensington Town Hall in London, at which the finalists were invited to present their reports before an assembled audience. All four finalists had submitted commendable reports, with the achievements they claimed being confirmed by independent vetting. All that remained was the final judgement. This needed to take into additional account their oral presentation and the credibility of their corporate accomplishments in the light of close questioning.

The eventual winners, by a unanimous decision, were the dustmen of Mansfield District Council. It may seem strange that garbage collectors should earn such a conspicuous place on the rostrum of glory and even more remarkable that their submission should surpass those of other worthy competitors. What is more, these dustmen showed remarkable self-confidence. Their bid to stay as contractors within the Council had been won following intense competition under the system of competitive compulsory tendering that prevailed at the time. They had risen to the occasion by meeting among themselves to consider how best they could operate a flexible service in a way that allowed them to offer a full range of guarantees. For their visit to London they wore Top Team T-shirts and had travelled down from Mansfield in a Rolls Royce, supplied by the Mayor, on the understanding that if they failed to win the award they would have to pay for the petrol. A driver of the dust-cart presented the report and he and his colleagues answered the questions fluently and with conviction. After the result was announced, the other competitors came forward and graciously congratulated the winners.

The first question this incident raises is why the dustmen of Mansfield District Council should perform so well as a team. Here the socio-economic background provides some clues. Some time before the competition was staged the area suffered the misfortune of mining closures. Many miners came on to the labour market at a time when few job openings were available. Since the Council was intent on replacing some of their unsuitable dustmen who were failing to provide a fully competitive service, some of the miners saw the vacancies created as an area of opportunity. The new recruits knew all about teamwork through their practical experience underground. Faced with hazards intrinsic to their work and dependent on co-operation demanded by the nature of their duties, teamwork had

8

for them a living meaning. This contrasts with other competitors in this national competition, who failed to make the shortlist, and were using teamwork in a contrived and artificial way. A typical entry would read like a department's annual report in which the employees are duly thanked. There was no sign of the social process in terms of which progress had been made. Towards the end of the report mention would be made of teamwork for the first time. Sometimes the word would not appear until the very last page, when it might recur several times.

That was not the only experience that began to sow doubt in my mind about the direction in which concepts about teamwork were heading. To an increasing extent training departments were engaged in running courses designed to promote the general values of teamwork. Usually exercises took the form of some joint activity carried out in an attractive and stimulating setting. The aim of these activities was seldom to discover some more effective mode of work. Rather the emphasis was on gaining insights into the behaviours and perceptions of other members of the group. Improved communication is a benefit that is always welcome, especially in organizations where people seldom talk to one another, and this clear outcome became one of the main advantages of attending this new set of training courses. Another commonly reported benefit was enjoyment. People who declare how much they enjoy a course also imply that the course itself is worthwhile. That may be pleasant news but indulgence in such satisfaction can also cause training to lose its focus.

Enjoyment in a social setting was being consciously used as a means of motivating employees. Such an objective in training becomes especially important in cultures where self-fulfilment takes precedence over demands on performance. Here I had reason to reflect on the time when a colleague and I had been invited to run a course for a large industrial corporation in the United States. This corporation had hitherto been run in an excessively authoritarian manner; as a consequence it had run into a downturn in its business. A newly appointed CEO now advocated a big culture switch. So the swing of the pendulum moved towards teamwork. The exercise we introduced was called teamopoly and was founded on the dynamics governing the well-known board game called Monopoly. In other words, success builds on success to create monopoly conditions, so creating huge advantages for those who get ahead. In this variant of the game, four people would operate as a team, complexity was widened, negotiation was given a wide measure of scope, and the rules were constructed in such a way that luck played only a small part in the eventual outcome. Hence there were winners and losers. At the conclusion of the exercise the team would analyse their strengths and weaknesses and, by examining the reasons for setbacks and failures, useful lessons could be learnt. In the past we had found that more was learned by teams that ran into difficulties than by winning teams who were prone merely to bask in self-congratulation!

However, in this particular setting the game did not work out according to plan. For the purpose of an initial trial the participants were drawn entirely from those working in the personnel field, with a softer approach to matters of human organization, and their immediate purpose was to assess the suitability of the course for their production and sales staff. In the event they did not like the competitive element and declared that they favoured exercises where 'everyone is a winner'. That was my first experience of an attitude I later perceived was becoming more widespread. Training was gravitating in its design towards the preferred comfort zone. Uncomfortable experiences, rather than becoming sources of learning, were interfering with the peace of mind of trainees. Training was conceived as a means of fostering team spirit, togetherness and human interaction: it was there to reinforce hopes and aspirations rather then to unsettle trainees or to change anything. As it happened, the soft regime that replaced the hard one proved to be short-lived. So that particular line appeared to be heading into a dead end.

Another linked problem is that training and educational courses, that offer great attractions in their own right, are inclined to generate difficulties in re-entry: 'I enjoyed myself so much on the course that I now realize how dull my job is'; 'The trainer proved so much nicer than my supervisor'; 'I have felt much more dissatisfied since my return'. To the extent that training courses develop their own internal criteria of success that differ, whether consciously realized or not, from the criteria that govern the body sponsoring the training, problems are always liable to arise.

The tendency for the indulgence factor to enter the equation is perhaps inevitable. It certainly happens in other fields. Take the way in which budgets earmarked for advertising and public relations are being spent in practice. Senior managers are often disposed to reserve boxes and expensive seats at leading sporting events and provide lavish entertainment for themselves and privileged others, including a few chosen clients and customers. There is usually no intention to change attitudes or perceptions or to secure new business. So also, some firms spend lavishly on away weekends for senior staff and their wives, thinly justified by notions of a conference embedded somewhere in the proceedings. In some cases decisions to stage pleasurable events are taken even before the means are found for financing them. Then discussion will focus on whether the planned occasion is covered more conveniently under a training or under an advertising budget. Self-indulgence has become a force operating wherever budgets are to be found.

That is not to deny that to spend a company's money by providing a welcome break for hard-pressed employees is a very worthy action, and it is notably absent in some countries where exploitation is rife. In the past, paternalistic employers in the UK were often disposed to stage an outing for their workers, especially before statutory holidays were introduced. Blackpool, in its early days, began as a centre of the holiday world as mill owners took their employees by coach to the seaside for the day. A pattern of pleasure for the workers was established which, in spite of package holidays to romantic places, continues there unabated today. There is clearly no moral reason why the directors of companies should not provide morale-boosting treats for themselves or their employees provided the finances of their companies can support such expenditure.

It is another matter, however, when human motives become so mixed that the indulgence factor intrudes into training and succeeds in side-tracking and obscuring its fundamental purpose. The risk is that focus may be lost. People are not being prepared in the basic skills of teamwork that generate more value from their joint endeavours. Instead, training is being lured towards group activities that are popular and become ends in themselves.

As proper teamwork began to lose its cutting edge, a new blandness came into being. Teamwork could imply that everyone was responsible. Equality of responsibility, with its total lack of social differentiation, could mean in effect that nobody

11

was responsible. Teamwork was beginning to lose its appeal. Such a condition inevitably excited a backlash and the counter-revolution soon led to a new crop of *dirigiste* management regimes. Such swings can happen almost overnight. As one chief executive is retired or dismissed and is replaced by another, much that has previously been accomplished is thrown out in favour of a new look. Misunderstanding the value and importance of team roles and of the very meaning of teams can put at risk years of development.

3

Distinguishing teams from groups

To the extent that teamwork was becoming a fashionable term, it began to displace the more usual reference to groups, including the *autonomous work group*, which was fast fading as a favoured term. Every group activity was now being described as 'teamwork'. Here one might be tempted to exclaim in Shakespearean mode: 'What's in a name? A rose by any other name would smell as sweet.' So does it matter whether one is talking about teams or groups?

The answer for those who have to make decisions is that it does. Group psychology is a field that exists in its own right. Large groups develop their own norms. A similar effect is found among sub-groups of some larger association. Strong forces operate on the collective psyche and compel young people, for example, to adopt particular forms of fashionable clothing, even when such clothing is obviously unsuitable for the conditions or for comfort. Such norms to conform exert their standardizing pull on individuals in the direction of whatever establishes group identity. Group psychology is not about co-operative role differentiation, as it is with teams; it is about planting a flag on common ground.

The confusion in vocabulary between the two terms *teams* and *groups* had to be addressed if the principles of good teamwork were to be retained and were not to be eroded by the thoughtless use of language. I therefore hit upon a simple way of expressing the difference between the two words. 'The *team*,' I would point out when addressing meetings of managers, 'is a term that management has borrowed from sport. Hierarchical structures throughout history have never used the word *team*. No such word would ever have slipped from the lips of Ghengis Khan.' I would go on to declare that the principles operating in sport applied equally well in management. I would then set people an exercise in which they were invited to find six characteristics that differentiated teams from groups.

The usual response from those who rose to the challenge was to come up with notions that were largely abstract in character. They might involve, for example, various forms of awareness or attitude or sense of purpose. 'But how would that help me, as an outsider, to spot the difference?' I would reply. There had to be a simpler means of making the distinction if teamwork were to be prevented from being sucked down into the conforming vortex of group work. So I set myself the problem of finding the best differentiator. After much thought, I decided the best lead lay with a simple four-letter word – *size*. Groups can comprise any number of people and, as numbers in the group increase, the identity and special role contribution of every individual member diminishes. Group identity and the herd instinct take over. Once that happens, group members look to the pack leader, as may be exemplified wherever mass political and religious rallies are held. A very different situation prevails when a few people with a shared objective meet together. Each one, ideally, will consider how best to contribute. Individuals then strive to find and stake out their personal identity within a social setting. In terms of behaviour, therefore, the *team* and the *group* exert opposite effects on their respective members.

If a team is smaller than a group, the qualifying question is: how small should small be? After many years of experience, I confess to having a favourite number for a team, which is four. The thinking here is that four people can each take one side of a square or rectangular table. There is no head of the table. The members are constrained to sit and, therefore, encouraged to act, by that seating arrangement, as a team. I am also fairly happy with five in number and content with six. After that number, the spread of contributions between members becomes more uneven and one person becomes more likely to dominate. As size increases, domination becomes linked increasingly with seniority and status, while merit in contribution plays a diminishing role. When a number of very senior people meet over and above the optimum size of team, so that a group situation prevails, *decibel management* now plays a significant part in the struggle for power. At that point a single powerful figure is likely to emerge as the recognized leader, a position reinforced by the deference shown by the other members.

The emphasis on the importance of size is consistent with the lessons that can be extracted from team sports. Every team will have its set size. The size allows each player a definite role to play in the team. There could not, of course, be thirty players in a football side or there would be chaos on the pitch. With too small a team on a pitch of a given size the players would soon be running around to the point of exhaustion. So for every field of activity there is an ideal number of players.

But on the question of size there is one important difference between a team activity in sport and one in which a number of people meet together to confer and decide. In the former instance the players may be dispersed on the field and, notably in the case of those on the wings, have little communication with one another during the course of play. In an industrial or public service context members of a team will be expected to be in constant communication with one another. The team is acting as a corporate body on which is positioned a corporate head. The problem about this head is that it houses several brains; they may not think alike and there is a limit to the numbers of brains that can pass the appropriate signals to the limbs of the body. When that happens there can be only two possibilities: either there is near total confusion or one of the brains takes over and the others have to be suppressed.

A decline in the clarity of group thinking had been brought to the fore through the researches of Irving Janis (see *Groupthink*, 1982, Houghton Mifflin, Boston, USA). In a well-documented study Janis was able to show how certain political and industrial fiascos had their roots in bad decision-making processes. He carefully noted the general character of its symptoms, which he called *groupthink*. They included illusions of unanimity and invulnerability, resort to stereotypes about out-groups, illusions about the superiority of the in-group and other recurring symptoms. While Janis has studied this phenomenon in great detail, the issue that claimed my attention was why the output of the whole should so poorly represent the capacity of its parts. Evidently this phenomenon was well established in the case of groups, but during the course of my career I had seldom encountered the same phenomenon in relation to teams.

The notable point about the studies of Janis is that senior people, who one might presume to be intelligent, were acting unintelligently in dealing with big issues. It was clearly a group phenomenon, manifesting itself only in group situations. It caused me to adopt the following working hypothesis: *any given group will act as though it has a group intelligence quotient which bears little relationship to the average intelligence quotient of its individual members.*

The issue now was to determine whether a forecast could be made of which groups would behave in this malfunctioning way. Here Janis offered no clear leads. I think the reason was that in the groups Janis studied no account was recorded of the numbers in the group. Such information may be of less importance where the emphasis is historical but is certainly needed when predictions have to be made. My experience of forays into forecasting had led me to believe that numbers are all-important. The most chaotic behaviour I have witnessed has always been in large groups that were supposed to be orderly. One is reminded of the saying '*A camel is a horse designed by a committee.*'

The importance of *size* had led me to develop an abstract connection between size and efficiency where this involved mental work (see Figure 2). Intelligence tends to show an immediate rise from the starting-point of one when small numbers of people confer and deliberate. As the saying goes, '*Two heads are better than one.*' Perhaps three are better than two and four may be better than three. After that, increasing numbers instead of adding something start to detract. That phenomenon is recognized by the increasing use of derogatory terms in the English language for describing larger groups such as mob and rabble.

After *size*, the next most important factor I consider to be *selection*. Here, as a starting-point, the football analogy is useful.

'If a football team consistently disappoints it supporters, what do they do?', I would ask those attending a workshop. There was no doubt about the reply: 'The fans would demand the dismissal of the manager', I would be told. 'But', I would object with feigned surprise, 'the manager isn't even playing.' Virtually no discussion was necessary. Everyone would understand the critical importance of the manager in selecting the team. Good results cannot be assured with the wrong players or with players who fail to combine well with each another. It is up to the manager, who selects the team, to get it right.

There are several other factors that characterize the difference between teams and groups (see Figure 3). In particular, issues of leadership and style are at the fore and show themselves as pulling in opposite directions. The quintessential feature of a small well-balanced team is that leadership is shared or rotates. As critical issues arise, different individuals come to the fore and make their special contribution. In the typical group, a very different situation prevails. The leadership stays unchanged in spite of the changing focus of the work, for solo leaders are not easily challenged or displaced. When solo leaders gain their ascendancy in a group they nearly always set out to standardize policies. They impose their own particular style and preferences on others. Dissenters are unwelcome. Inner tensions are released through external expression, while any lingering hostility is now deflected towards outsiders.

The sequence of events then is that large groups typically throw up solo leaders. An autocratic style ensues, which eventually turns into an autocratic regime. If the majority come to regret the consequences, one response is to change the leader. So the revolution arrives. In history that has happened many times, but it usually only means that one tyrant replaces another, since the original sequence of events is reactivated. The change that can be guaranteed to give surer results is to turn groups into teams. That offers the assurance that there can be no team tyranny, for by its very nature power is diffused once it is distributed within a team.

However, such a change requires a fundamental social revolution. It is unlikely to happen without a new emphasis on education and democratization, assisted by the due passage of time. Meanwhile, in most organizations the oscillations between teams and groups will continue. Leaders with high personal ambitions will try to impose themselves. Their strategy will be to do away with teams and to place themselves at the head of groups, amorphous in character and therefore susceptible to assimilating the outlook of the leader. The best way to ensure that this does not happen is to construct jobs round a network of individuals and teams and as far as possible to do away with groups as the basic building blocks of organization.

Chapter

4

Understanding work roles

People in teams have not been brought together merely to engage in social relationships: they are there to perform a body of work. This will have a bearing on the sort of roles they take up. Work roles may be defined as the mix of tasks and responsibilities undertaken by individuals or executed within teams. Team roles signify the contributions that individuals are typically disposed to make in their working relationships: they are part of the input to the job. Work roles, by focusing on the *demands* of the job, in a language designed for ease of communication, offer the prospect that the *inputs* and *outputs* are brought together in a more equable balance.

Here the reader may ask: why should such issues have become so important at the time of the new millennium? At earlier periods in human history less demanding situations could lend themselves to simpler solutions. In pre-industrial societies work was of lower complexity and the conventional division of labour by gender, age and social status met the needs of the time. However, with the coming of industry the distribution of work according to past patterns became a restricting factor. Large numbers of workers were now needed on factory sites embracing a growing number of distinctive jobs. These came to be classified according to the trade skills required. The definition of a trade would not only relate to apprenticeship and training but also would commonly cover the tools used. So, in practice, one tradesman would not touch the tools of another. Such observance of protocol had obvious convenience at the time. The disadvantages inherent in such an arrangement were ignored. Exactly where the boundary lay between jobs might seem a matter of only minor concern when jobs were plentiful. But, in times of recession, what had once seemed a useful measure in clear-cut job definition opened the way for demarcation disputes. Trouble started once the various parties that straddled job borderlines faced the reality that jobs were beginning to disappear. While fear of job insecurity might increase attachment to traditional practices, the practices themselves were being steadily undermined by the pressures of increasing competition. The model for dividing jobs strictly according to trades was becoming outmoded. Basing a job on one particular occupational or trade skill has a limiting effect on the efficiency of work practices. Irregularities in workflow inevitably occur in the distribution of work activities between different jobs. Firmly set demarcation boundaries mean that flexibility is lost and workers become less generally employable.

In response to that shortcoming, another form of division of labour came into being with the aim of distributing work more evenly. Work could be taken as a quantum – studied, measured and assessed. It meant that a new job would be created only when an employer could find enough work content to justify its existence. As a result, jobs changed from being originally conceived as the activities of a trade to becoming a collection of necessary work inputs appropriate to the current state of demand for outputs. Multi-skilling, in this context, offered huge benefits in labour productivity. Yet, at the same time it generated a new set of problems. In a versatile labour force everyone in theory could be called on to do anything. So who decides who should do what and when?

One possibility was the autonomous work group. The group itself would have to decide. But unfortunately, as the last chapter showed, groups do not work efficiently. They lack the structure needed for decision-making or their members tend to coalesce in a way that cultivates groupthink. In some cases such laxity in organization invites the entry of a single dominant figure so that the group then forms its own self-constructed hierarchy. In that case it reverts to a traditional organizational form and the wheel has turned full circle. That is broadly the essence of the contemporary crisis.

The problem now to be faced was that, while we had established that teams were more productive than groups and had developed a useful language of inputs designed to facilitate the working relationships of team members, there was still a need for a common language that could give expression to work demands and to their associated work outputs. Team roles may deal with what individuals are disposed to contribute. That was a big step forward. But the question still had to be asked: to what end? Those ends had to reflect the requirements of the external world. Under the current mode of transmission, demands were either being presented as lists of items, without any form of arrangement or prioritization, or at the other end of the spectrum as simple goals, which left everyone guessing about how best to proceed. It was only hierarchy that could be relied on to turn formal demands into orderly progression, which was why so many socially conceived paradigms for setting up work were proving shortlived.

The general uncertainty about the proper nature of jobs showed itself conspicuously in accident or pollution disasters, or indeed where anything went conspicuously wrong. Then enquiry would reveal confusion and misunderstandings about where responsibility lay. That was not surprising because work roles had never been expressed in terms of responsibilities, or where that term had been used, people were not clear what it meant. At the time I was conscious of a chain of recurring disasters in the medical field, for which responsibility was difficult to establish. The complications had their roots in the paradox that, while patients *belong* to given consultants and medical directors, the diseases and ailments don't know that they belong: they cross departmental boundaries at will. It was generally accepted in most organizations that some responsibilities need to be shared, while others are suitable for being discharged by particular people. Yet few know which are of one type and which are of another. Even more serious is the failure of many to see the difference between a responsibility and a task. A task is a necessary item of work that has to be performed; a responsibility is a goal or an objective for which a person or persons are held accountable. Since I had occasion to speak to

21

gatherings of managers from time to time, I thought it worthwhile to make the distinction between these two very different roles that feature in work.

However, I soon faced objections from discussants. It was pointed out to me that some tasks are so important that they should only be given to a responsible person. When that happens, a jobholder is undertaking a responsibility. So, in effect, it would be argued there is no fundamental difference between a task and a responsibility. Even Peter Drucker's well-regarded book *Management, Tasks, Responsibilities, Practices* (Butterworth-Heinemann, reprinted 1999) fails to define the difference between a task and a responsibility. The reason no doubt is that the distinction can be assumed. But it cannot. In due course I was to discover that *responsibility* is used in common parlance in three different ways. In one sense it refers to *the sense of moral responsibility* – a desired attribute in any employee. In another sense it denotes *span of control* – a means of measurement that allows an appropriate level of remuneration to be calculated under job evaluation (see also Chapter 8). Here a larger span correlates with a larger number of people supervised or a higher cost in the capital equipment for which a person is in charge. In a third sense responsibility signifies *being accountable for an outcome* – typically covering managerial accountability where discretion is left to the person as to how a desired and agreed outcome is to be achieved.

It was this experience that made me realize how easily words can become a barrier to communication. Such a conclusion is supported by referring to the *Oxford English Dictionary* on the meanings of selected words in common usage. The range of meanings and nuances in meanings would surprise many. It brought home in a general way what was already becoming apparent in the case of much favoured buzz words: how frequently terms like leadership, teamwork and competence are freely used to convey quite different notions, leaving everyone nodding their heads in agreement when in reality there is no agreement. Now add to this problem the linguistic differences to be found in multinational companies or in localities that house immigrant minorities, and the scope for wide misunderstandings becomes plain.

It seemed there could be only one way out of the problem, which was to replace words as the primary form of communication. In turn their place could be taken by colour (see Figure 4). The advantage of colour is that it can transmit meaning without any form of oral expression. All core work in a job could be classified in four types. There were prescribed tasks that had to be performed by a particular person in a particular way (Blue work). There was work involving personal responsibility, for the results of which the individual was personally accountable (Yellow work). There were tasks that could be performed in a variable way that took account of circumstances (Green work). And finally there was responsibility, involving decision-making, that needed to be shared by several people, as in a team (Orange work).

The choice of the colours was important, for they needed to act as cues as to what was required. Colour can be distractive when first used, for to many it signifies emotional mood or political attachment. Therefore the colours had to be meaningful if their communication was to be accepted. Blue, we reasoned, was the language of tradition and could be associated with the formal means of dispensing instructions. Blue was the colour of the sea and when sailing all things need to be 'shipshape'. Yellow recommended itself for its initial letter Y, a stem with two arms. It is up to You, another Y, to choose between the two arms as to which direction you will take. Green is universally recognized as the colour of the environment. How a task is to be performed should take account of immediate circumstances. Orange is a fruit, as well as a colour, and this fruit is round, as should be the shape of the table at which a well-balanced team meets to confer.

We thought that explanation simple enough to be readily comprehended by both managers and workers. In our first pilot trial we decided to compare how given jobs appeared to both parties, including estimates on how time was distributed between the various components of the job. The estimate of the manager was not revealed to the jobholder and in due course the two sets of estimates were compared. The general picture to emerge was that managers saw much of the job as being Blue work. If the jobholders did it correctly they would get a correct result. The jobholders presented a different picture to the investigators. They saw themselves as having a larger proportion of Yellow work and believed the managers did not understand the level of responsibility or decision-making that was involved. A further notable point was that the two groups used different vocabularies in describing much the same work. With these two different perceptions the communication link between the two parties tended to be tenuous. From the point of view of the investigators, the attempt to see how far the two perceptions of the job diverged or were in accord was becoming excessively time-consuming.

We now decided on a change of plan. The framing of the work role would in future comprise contributions by both the manager and the jobholder. The manager would set out the core work and the jobholder would be asked to assign the proportion of time spent on the various components of the core work presented. But now, in addition, the jobholder was given scope in another direction. Under new terms of reference the jobholder was asked to describe any further work entered into *beyond* the core work, so offering up a catalogue of additional work executed during the course of the job. Again, the jobholder was asked to estimate the proportion of time spent on these items.

We examined the nature of these items and concluded that they fell into three categories. The first category comprised activities that related to the core work but had never been specified. For example, fetching materials in short supply might not have been mentioned as part of the job but would be voluntarily undertaken by a person with any initiative. Helping out others or dealing with unexpected visitors might again occupy an appreciable amount of time without ever being recognized as part of the job itself. Had they been specified as part of the job, they would have been recorded as Green work – but they were not. Hence the jobholder would be expanding the job by incorporating items perceived as making a useful contribution. This grey area surrounding the core work we considered should carry the title of Grey, a colour that is indefinite yet acts as a good background to other brighter colours.

The second category was also a means of contributing more to the job, but it was less reactive and more innovative in character. Sometimes a jobholder would find a more effective way of carrying out some aspect of the work, even putting it into operation without authority. For example, files might be reorganized; a new useful supplier might be noted and contacted. That could be time well spent. Yet it could also spell dangers. If such initiatives are to cause a job to grow in a positive direction, the jobholder would need to communicate upwards to the manager in order to check that there would be no adverse side-effects.

Orthodox personnel systems make little provision for engaging in that type of activity. We needed to find a name to convey its nature. The name we decided on was White work. The image here is of starting with a blank piece of paper on which is then written something fresh, unsolicited and unexpected.

The third category of work in which jobholders engaged comprised items perceived by them to be neither useful nor productive. In the eyes of the jobholder these activities contributed nothing but were time-consuming. It is plain that most people do not like wasting time. They find it especially hard to endure when they feel their time is being wasted by someone else. And so there came to be revealed a form of work activity which had not previously been identified: it was, in effect, an oxymoron – a work activity that is not work. The jobholder believes it to be valueless but it is something from which escape is not possible. A typical example is form-filling, which serves no evident end. Other examples will be presented in the chapter that follows and the whole question will be examined as to why people should be busy engaging in the valueless use of time. The name eventually chosen for this activity was Pink work. Here Pink conjured up a picture of pink elephants and pink panthers; in other words, it referred to imaginary work.

Our pilot studies had revealed then seven categories of work activity. Four were those that could be demanded (ideally) by the purveyors of work. On to that core work the jobholder could add three further categories of work activity. So the importance of the message could be summarized as follows. To gain a proper perspective of work roles in their most effective mode of operation we need to understand how the manager can best communicate the core of the job. Yet equally important is how the jobholder communicates to the manager what more the job can deliver and what parts of the job, as at present constituted, contribute nothing of value.

The pilot trials taught us to conceive of work roles as being cast in a dynamic system, addressing the demands of the job, while striving to deliver more of value. If jobs are to live and earn their place in an ever-changing world, they must grow and develop; and here the structures from the past often act as impediments.

5

What Pink work reveals

Work expands to fill the time available for its completion. Parkinson's Law is famed for its simple truth. An elderly retired aunt will spend all day writing a postcard and posting it to her niece, just as a recession will still leave office workers ever-busy handling papers and engaged in numerous telephone conversations. Whatever the basic cause may be, there is nothing new about people spending their time wastefully. That very fact presents opportunities. A lasting impression from the early days of my industrial career was that work study experts were kept busy studying and measuring unproductive and unoccupied time. The savings they could recommend were derived from using what they could reveal as available time to greater advantage. This approach offered a proven formula for raising the productivity of workers.

The question now to be posed is whether Pink work is merely an expression of Parkinson's Law in a colourful form. Yet, in spite of some obvious similarities, I must reject the notion that the two conditions are co-terminous. In fact they scarcely overlap. It is true they both deal with time wasted, but the two conditions spring from quite different sources. The Parkinsonian wastage of time is intended by the person involved, even if the process is subconscious. Take the office where work is slack. There is nothing so tedious as doing nothing. One recurring finding from studies of secretarial functions is that the most unpopular jobs are those where there is too little work. It follows that one solution open to anyone in that situation is to engage in an activity that appears industrious. The simulation can be so effective that the boss believes that what he or she perceives as work really is so, and that the staffing level of the office is about right. Clearly it is in the interest of workers wishing to retain their jobs to appear to be shouldering a proper work load, or even one that is on the heavy side. A general complicity among those who work in close association to support that impression finishes the picture. When a boss walks through an office, heads are down, with noses close to paper or keyboard, while serious intentions are conveyed by the frowns of those embroiled in conversations on the telephone. As the boss leaves the room, heads come up and people start talking to each another again.

A very different situation arises when Pink work is reported. The jobholder is in effect complaining about his or her time being wasted. Very often the boss is the source of the Pink work, in which case the complaint would almost certainly not be aired publicly without some probing. In any case, jobholders are reluctant to cite examples of Pink work until their confidence can be won over. In their mind, the wasted time being forced upon them and which they are being asked to expose risks being mistaken for the time they deliberately waste and need to disguise. That was very evident when comparing the reactions of jobholders being interviewed at their place of employment, in connection with the application of work-role systems. Pink work would be treated as though it was strange and unfamiliar. There was a very different reaction from participants attending an externally located educational workshop. In the case of the latter, I would divide the assembled gathering into separate groups of four, five or six people and invite one person at each group table to furnish from their work experience an example of Pink work. The usual problem was to limit each table to only one contribution. Examples abounded and they were often reported with glee. Clearly for some it was a relief to expose shortcomings that it would have been unwise to mention at their place of employment. Those attending educational workshops do not feel vulnerable and they can speak their minds freely.

To replicate this situation in the workplace it has proved advantageous to use a trained facilitator in order to elicit a frank response from the jobholder. *'Did you have to spend time on anything that did not contribute to your work objectives?'* invites a chance to grumble. The better the listener, the more is poured out. The waste of time that is revealed exonerates the jobholder from any sense of blame because the source is external to the person. Here it is important for the facilitator to show how this information can be used constructively through eventual changes in systems and procedures. A climate is then created in which reporting Pink work is viewed as a service rather than an unauthorized disclosure which makes the person reporting the Pink work feel vulnerable.

Pink work has now been recorded from a variety of locations and situations. Sometimes the reaction to this news of wasted time, hitherto unreported, is so dramatic that it sets in motion major organizational changes. Such was the situation in Sweden when a combined programme of team roles and work roles was introduced into the Swedish Prison Service. Hitherto the Service had operated through a centralized system of management located in Stockholm. Delayering in the number of management levels had had the effect of removing much of the discretionary element from the jobs of prison officers. In place of discretionary powers they were now burdened with a great deal of centralized administration. One example of this burden was that a large amount of required information was periodically taken into a particular prison office where it was stacked and disregarded. After a due interval the accumulated information would be destroyed. This wasteful procedure was soon identified by the prison officers as Pink work, and its disclosure prompted a major change in the way in which the Prison Service was run.

Many different types of Pink work have been revealed in our studies, but already certain patterns are becoming very evident and recurring (see Figure 5). Seven of these will be listed, of which the first three are grouped together because they all relate to the use of information. In an age in which information is at a premium and is easily stored and retrieved in computers, information-gathering has run amok.

Pink work number 1 is the collection of redundant information. The same information is available elsewhere or has been collected in parallel by another person. One of the examples cited to us related to a firm that had made an early use of IT systems in its management. Nevertheless, the original paperwork system continued and took up much time. Upon enquiry it was revealed that it duplicated information already available on the Intranet. Investigation into how this paperwork had survived showed that it had originally served a purpose as a safety back-up when the computer system was new. Yet it was still there twelve years later!

Pink work number 2 concerns requests for information that is never used. The most common form of this relates to reports. Reports take some time to write. They are often used as background material to enable decisions to be made. Before they are completed, handed in and read, the decision is made. So the reports serve no purpose and the writer is left with a sense of deep frustration. Some bosses are very prone to demand special reports but are equally prone to make sudden unexpected journeys so they are never available to read them. Demands for special information and a proclivity for making premature and macho-like decisions are unhappy companions.

Pink work number 3 relates to information that is marginal and judged not to be cost-effective in its collection. At one time the information was used but now other forms of information provide better leads. Nevertheless, the old information continues in case someone finds it useful. In such a situation cancellation almost never takes place. Where there are multiple users of information, as with medical community work or social case work, number 3 type Pink work flourishes.

Pink work number 4 refers to waiting-time or more specifically to unplanned waiting-time. 'Why are we waiting?' soon becomes the refrain of those whose work is held up by the expected arrival that fails to materialize. The inevitable frustration is perhaps at its strongest among those waiting for medical records or X-rays at critical moments. A variant is where the records that have arrived do not correspond with what is required. However, Pink waiting-time is most prevalent in the world of the manual worker. Waiting for materials to arrive on building sites is a common plague of the building industry and has been closely associated with bankruptcies in small building firms. Similarly, Pink work figures among operatives in manufacturing industry as a result of shortage of supplies and components. This often results simply from the failure within a factory to make timely deliveries from stores. At other times the failure is associated with outside suppliers. A lorry has been delayed by traffic congestion on the motorway or a faulty batch has had to be returned. The effects of mishaps of this nature have been made more critical by the wide adoption of Just-in-Time policies. Buffer stocks have previously served a just-in-case purpose and their elimination invites Pink work. Any removal of unnecessary waiting-time demands better planning and co-ordination. In this context the role of Pink work in reporting and identifying the problem makes an important contribution to progress.

Pink work number 5 could be described as empty antics. Set procedures are followed as a result of policies that do not and cannot produce any useful work output. A typical case is the advertising of appointments when decisions have already been made. The claim may be made in the spirit of public pride that all appointments are advertised, but acting on the letter rather than in the proclaimed spirit wastes time and money, puts people to a great deal of trouble, and is a deception. Empty antics have begun to figure in the field of quality control. Procedures of no evident value are followed according to the formal requirements of BS 9000. The aim is to imply that high quality is assured, whereas attention to known sources of trouble is delayed in the interests of gaining contract approval. Empty antics are especially resented by conscientious professionals who are keen to do a good job.

Pink work number 6 covers an activity that on the surface looks inseparable from real work. That factor is travelling. Area representatives may be required to meet a certain quota of visits; the intention is to ensure they work hard enough. Some of these calls they know to be abortive, but they will go through the motions, using up fuel and time, when they know that the more effective action would be to telephone first. The instruction to make a certain number of visits is an example of what happens when a job is set up as Blue work. If the job were set up as Yellow work the area representative would be made accountable for some business outcome. He or she would decide how many visits would be likely to produce the desired results. In general, the over-emphasis on treating a job as Blue work is one of the main generators of Pink activities.

Pink work number 7 arises in meetings. I have left this topic until last, so that it may be regarded as the climax of this chapter. My experience is that meetings are quoted as the main source of Pink work by between 60 and 70 per cent of those attending executive workshops. A possible reason is that executives spend much of their time at meetings. In contrast operatives will spend little or no time at meetings, so their source of Pink work is different. However, changes in the nature of manpower in industry and the public services mean that there will be relatively fewer operatives in the future in comparison with the growing numbers of executives and professional personnel. Pink meetings are therefore likely to grow, unless something can be done about them.

The first need is to distinguish between meetings that are Pink and those that are Orange. To some extent this represents the difference between those that are well conceived, well prepared and well conducted and those that are not. However, that is not the only difference. Those who emerge from a meeting commonly react to it in different ways. Active participants who have played a due part in formulating decisions will see the occasion as a good example of Orange work. On the other hand, anyone who has been present, has not been consulted and has said nothing is likely to give a Pink verdict. Here it may be argued that whoever convened and presided at the meeting is at fault for not drawing the inactive person into the process. But often there is more to it than that. Those who are well chosen can turn a potentially poor meeting into a success. Equally, there are some who will never thrive in meetings, find them onerous and feel they are a diversion from more important work. A lead as to which people are likely to thrive and which would rather withdraw is usually indicated from their respective team roles. Co-ordinators and Resource investigators are often fond of meetings, while also being useful contributors. Teamworkers acquiesce in meetings but will go with the flow. Monitor evaluators only like focused meetings that are devoid of trivia. Plants see meetings as occasions to offer favoured messages but otherwise don't like them. Implementers and Completers only like meetings that deal with practical issues. Shapers like meetings they can dominate but otherwise think them a waste of time. And finally Specialists dislike all meetings that deal with business outside their own particular speciality.

The success of meetings therefore depends in part on who is invited to them. But to find a firmer guarantee that meetings will not degenerate into a heavy shade of Pink, some principles need to be formulated about the shape and purpose of meetings. I have long sensed the need for this, as I have been aware that there is no general theory of meetings. Those guidelines that do exist treat meetings as though they belong to some homogenous body to which some uniform set of rules can be applied. Therefore the whole scene needs to be re-examined and, in view of the importance of eliminating Pink work, it is timely that this matter should be considered in the next chapter.

6

A framework for meetings

If meetings are a prime source of Pink work, should they not be abolished? Time could then be used more effectively. Clearly, that is not the conclusion we should reach. Meetings are held for a purpose. They are essential in the case of Orange work for dealing with complex strategic and policy issues.

While some meetings serve a legitimate and important purpose, the case for other meetings is often marginal or worse. There is some evidence to suggest that meetings can occur as compensation for lack of clarity in the construction of jobs: with no clear mandate people hesitate to engage in any proactive activity. The only way to decide anything is to have a meeting. Formless organizations also cherish meetings in the absence of any clear reporting relationships or clear statement of responsibilities. Meetings also exist for social reasons. They counter the sense of exclusion and anonymity. They satisfy the ethical needs of those who believe that everyone is entitled to personal involvement.

If we restrict our attention to work roles, and see meetings as a means of accomplishing work, the subject opens itself up for a clear line of attack. The first move must be to separate team meetings from group meetings along the lines set out in Chapter 3. Team meetings promise creativity and purposeful decision-making; group meetings have more to do with information and its transmission in an environment conducive to establishing social norms and compliance. The two purposes are basically different and this difference between the two types should always be borne in mind, if the pattern of one is not to confuse the conduct of business in the other.

Studying Pink work provides useful evidence about what should not be done. But it prompts the need to start at the other end and to establish what makes a great meeting. Here I have chosen to retrace certain events where the outcome is known. Whenever I have stumbled upon a new product in a company that has proved a success, or come across an innovative strategy that moved a company in a new positive direction, I have seen that as the opportunity to ask the question 'How did it start?'

A general impression is that the bigger the outcome the smaller the starting-point. The word strategy, taken from the Greek, refers to a military general. The general draws up a plan of attack, which is then passed down the line and put into effect by the troops. The implication here is that the general thinks and decides; he is the chess player controlling the pieces on the board, which are moved around at will. The image, however, is different from the effective reality. There is general recognition that 'two brains are better than one'. The general may decide but he and his staff officers discuss; and a decision will follow from that discussion. Moving from the military, of which I have limited knowledge, to the industrial, with which I am more familiar, retrospective study shows that major strategy initiatives have usually started with discussions between two or three people. Perhaps surprisingly, most of those discussions have not originated in formal settings. Discussions appear to have started in corridors, at the bar in a pub, or in a restaurant, or even on holiday. Here there is some justification for the away weekend or the development event held in a remote and attractive location. In such a relaxing environment it is easier to produce a break in thought.

A break in strategy has much in common with the generation of a new idea. But ideas do not necessarily lead to innovation. A single idea, unsupported, seldom achieves anything of substance. The scene is best set for innovation when one idea comes up across another in an adjacent field; when one idea is juxtaposed against some fact or consideration that has previously been left out of account. The social setting therefore plays an important part in moving forward the germ of an idea – but it is not *any* social setting. Inevitably people interact with some better than with others. That is no doubt why informal groupings tend to figure prominently on these occasions. In effect, people select the partners with whom they wish to discuss a promising possibility.

A creative team, or rather one designed in the hope that it will be creative, raises some different issues. It will not be a spontaneous gathering. Someone will have put it together – and the design may be faulty. The selection of the players will be as critical as in a sports team. The danger is that some membership will be ex officio and may include a well-qualified person who will ruin the team atmosphere. The intended creative team will be at risk if it is dominated even by some star player, who is reluctant to pass the ball, just as in a sports team. If leadership is to play a role, it should rotate. Leadership is best shared between different contributors; each will recognize when his or her turn has come and when another is best fitted to take over. In that way the spontaneous dynamism of the team will be retained.

When project teams are set up, a different situation prevails. There will be more constraints and good reasons why particular individuals, often with special technical knowledge, will need to be present, irrespective of their personal characteristics. Initially the team may look unbalanced in terms of team-role contributions. That lack of balance may, however, be corrected when the finishing touches are put to the team and the final placements are made. Project teams need to be handled in a firmer and more disciplined way than creative teams. A project leader will need to be appointed who possesses not only the necessary personal qualities but the knowledge and authority that can gain the respect of the team members.

While project teams may emphasize knowledge and problem-solving abilities, operational planning in contrast calls for the co-ordination of people engaged in miscellaneous tasks. It is at this point that the word team should be dropped. Task-focused groups will attend meetings on the basis of the jobs on which they are engaged. There will be no further element of selection. The person who conducts the meeting will not need any outstanding knowledge but will be expected to demonstrate skills in linking people who in the normal course of events would be unlikely to communicate with each other.

Some meetings arise because new goals and targets are set and have to be announced. Some time will also need to be set aside for discussion. Here the formula that served the Roman army for hundreds of years, and was part of its structure, still applies. The ideal size for a group under a commander was considered to be ten. Not only did it facilitate a roll call of those present (on the fingers of each hand), but spoken communication was possible at normal voice level. Above that number, a new remoteness could change relationships between a commander and the commanded.

Larger meetings encompass people who belong to different units. Inter-departmental meetings need to be conducted with great care and diplomacy by the person in charge. One problem is that of gaining respect from those who come from different backgrounds. Here formalities and a set agenda aid the process and avert conflict among those with differing interests. Someone of recognized seniority with good co-ordination skills is best fitted to conduct meetings of that nature.

Still larger meetings place their spotlight on the important leader who will have convened the meeting with a special purpose in view. Such meetings are suitable for formal announcements and are unsuitable for discussion and debate.

The gradation of meetings according to size and purpose is inseparably linked with the way in which the meetings themselves are conducted. In general, work is more evenly spread the smaller the meeting, so offering a high participation rate. In a large meeting all the input is likely to be made by a single person – that explains why larger meetings are commonly seen as sources of Pink work. Few people, other than disciples, wish to be harangued by someone who cannot be answered.

The conference is perhaps the only meeting of any size where the prime purpose is unconnected with the nature of the leadership. Ostensibly, the reason for attending a conference is to present a paper or to hear presentations from those with a distinguished professional reputation. The reality is that most people attend conferences to meet colleagues with whom they can exchange opinions and share experiences. The conference hall, along with its antechambers, is the place where those who wish to meet each other can congregate. It will not matter much if individuals fail to take their seats in the hall, preferring to talk outside instead, for once people have registered, there is no roll call. There is no compulsion to attend as absence will not be noticed. The conference is the only form of meeting where truancy is acceptable. It is through truancy that important business is conducted. The larger the conference, the more important it becomes for individuals to focus on meeting other participants. Hence, leadership at a conference takes on a secondary role. The conference chairperson will be chosen for professional reputation, often acting as little more than a figurehead. Conferences do not accord with the general principles applying to meetings because the micro-meetings occurring within them usually have greater significance than the macro-meeting itself.

There are some people who have adopted a negative stance towards meetings in general in the realization that sitting round a table talking to people, while under the pretence of doing business, is a congenial way of spending time. If that is the case, such activity should be discouraged. Archie Norman, Chairman of ASDA, is said to have no chairs or tables in his meetings so that no one can waste time. As a result, business, it is claimed, is dealt with swiftly.

However, in a world where many interfaces arise between different groups and issues of complexity abound, the presumption must be made that meetings will continue to play an essential role in modern life. If that is recognized, the objective must be to extract as much value as possible from each meeting and to eliminate practices that can lead to waste. A format for meetings in their ideal form according to their intended purpose is set out in Figure 6. As a general guide, the larger the meeting the smaller the time-span that should be allotted to it, if Pink work is to be avoided. In contrast, meetings attended by only a few people and covering major matters need not be hurried. Small meetings are economic in their use of personnel time, especially if set up according to the principles of Orange work.

A classification of ten different types of meeting and an understanding of their separate purposes and modes of conduct are prerequisites for putting meetings to effective use (see

Figure 6). The boundaries I have set out are seldom observed. Instead there is a drift towards general-purpose meetings that occupy an indefinite time-span. Then form and discipline are lost, talk-shops result and nobody listens. The antithesis also happens – everybody listens (or makes a pretence of listening) and only one person talks and to little avail. In either of these extreme cases no worthwhile work is likely to ensue and meetings take on the bright hue of Pink.

Chapter

7

Whatever happened to empowerment?

Favoured words come and go in the vocabulary of managers and professionals in the personnel field. Empowerment provides just such an example. One hears less of the word these days than one did formerly. The concept of empowerment certainly implies some radical reappraisal of work roles and so falls within the terms of reference of this book. Hence there seems a need to check on the current standing of the concept and, if anything has gone wrong with what looked a promising development, to ascertain what the reason might be.

The most definitive writing on empowerment I judge to be *The Art of Empowerment* by Ron Johnson and David Redmond (FT and Pitman Publishing, London, 1998). These authors depict empowerment as the pinnacle of employee involvement, occurring at the end of a chain in social participation. That evolution is seen as taking place in five successive steps: informing before consulting, consulting before sharing, sharing before delegating and finally full empowerment itself. At each stage, managers and workers will be testing each other in terms of honesty, openness and trustworthiness. Empowerment requires a high level of commitment and is reached through this process of growing trust. In a private communication Ron Johnson expresses the view that levels of empowerment can vary between departments within the same organization. As time goes on levels of empowerment can progressively increase.

Trust and openness are difficult concepts to measure and assess. Many companies consider they create a friendly atmosphere and that a great deal of consultation takes place. But consultation is all too often seen in mechanistic terms – as comprising a form of communication that hinges on information technology. The authors of *The Art of Empowerment* cite the following:

> *An organization specializing in IT had two different parts to its operation. One part specialized in providing in-depth consultancy, helping organizations to draw up specifications for computer systems. The other part provided an ongoing support service to similar organizations. Often staff from one part of the organization would pick up information that could provide leads for the other part, but these were infrequently passed on to those who could make use of them.*
>
> *Initially, the organization thought to solve this by setting up complicated communications systems to facilitate this exchange of information. They came to realize, however, that the need was not for better systems, but for:*
>
> - *better understanding between people in the two arms of the organization*
> - *more commitment to the organization as a whole*
>
> *Front line staff needed to appreciate and understand the needs of their colleagues in other areas of work. They also needed to recognize that their futures were tied up with the success of the organization as a whole, not just with their own particular jobs and sections. (p. 19)*

The authors believe that organizations need better, quicker decisions at all levels. A crucial question therefore is whether a given work-culture can develop an appropriate mode of decision-making. My investigations into both these areas led me to postulate that work cultures and the focal points of decision-making can be treated separately within an organization and represented in broad though distinctive descriptions.

Organizations differ from one another in three clear-cut forms of basic decision-making. There are organizations dominated by a top-person, who puts his personal stamp on every significant decision. There are organizations where decisions are made by small circles: a few key executives operate together in their own independent way. And thirdly there is consultation and consensus: decisions emerge through a social process that may be sophisticated or at times convoluted. I would also have to admit that in some organizations the decision-making process is obscure, not only in my eyes but in the eyes of many employees.

As far as work culture is concerned my focus fell on how work was distributed. Here again there were three evident patterns. Employees were placed in structured jobs expressed in terms of job specifications and job descriptions; in effect, people had clear boundaries around well-defined work. In a second pattern, objectives were given to employees and the rest was left to them. A third pattern placed the emphasis on the assimilation of the individual into the work group. Group members then distribute work among themselves. Finally, there were some organizations in which there was no clear pattern: people were thrown in and left to fend for themselves.

Since empowerment requires a particular form of work culture and leads to a characteristic mode of decision-making, it seemed important to see how far the necessary conditions were present among the representatives of companies attending the seminars at which I was an invited speaker. The method I adopted was to present the four categories (including the uncertain ones) along these two separate dimensions and to ask participants to select the one of the sixteen boxes available that best described the current position in the organization from which they came.

My expectation was that the more rigid type of work culture would be associated with a more authoritarian type of decision-making. As the results came in, I was surprised to find that the association was much less close than I had supposed. There were entries in nearly every one of the sixteen boxes. General patterns were difficult to detect. Could these results have come about through random distribution, I wondered. Could the participants have been uncertain about which box to select for their entries? The only way was to find out by discussion. My conclusion was that participants had genuinely sought to represent how their

41

companies operated. They amplified their points by examples and anecdotes. As a result of the information they furnished, I was able to place a general description on each of the sixteen boxes (see Figure 7 and Table 7.1).

The most favoured boxes were those relating to Competitive Individualism (giving rise to fragmented efforts), Competitive Cabals and Layered Teamwork. Strangely, the box deemed most appropriate to Team Empowerment was the only one not represented by chosen entries. The most likely interpretation was that the general conditions conducive to its emergence were lacking. In other words, either the cultural forms were absent or the favoured mode of decision-making would have conflicted with any attempt to make empowerment effective.

Upon reflection, I realized that the only cases where I knew that Team Empowerment had been a success involved the services of an experienced and well-reputed consultant. The more I thought about that fact the clearer became the explanation in the light of our pilot attempts to introduce work roles and its associated software into industry. The intermediary role had proved crucial. Communication top-down was always a straightforward matter, but when the communication chain was reversed, a great deal of lubrication was needed to get it to happen at all. Workers are reluctant to express themselves frankly other than to their peers. Nor do they expect to carry real responsibility; decisions are for bosses. And even when responsibility is devolved, it can be misread as a sign of weakness from above. Misunderstandings are rife between different levels in a hierarchy because they do not communicate as though on an equal footing. The inter-mediary is there as an independent person to educate, encourage and, if need be, to arbitrate. Then results can flow – and they can be spectacular in their accomplishment.

However, there is a further impediment on the road to empowerment. There is some general confusion as to what empowerment means. Does it mean that all responsibility is passed over from a manager to a particular person or to a team? Such a shift would be tantamount to abdication. A manager must retain some responsibility. An empowered team will have some responsibility too. But how are the two responsibilities to be divided? Whatever emerges will come about as a result of an evolutionary process involving a period of negotiation. Effective

Table 7.1 Explanation of items in boxes (see Figure 7)

---

1 One person runs a well-defined organization and takes personal control. Job definitions ensure that employees act in a regulated way

2 In a formal organization heads of departments run their own establishments and only meet when they come together at a senior level. As the senior meetings are likely to be limited in effectiveness, much depends on how personal empires operate

3 Decision-making is diffuse. Individuals sit as functional representatives on various committees to formulate policies. Action is slowed down accordingly

4 The emphasis is on following formal and well-established procedures. The regularity of business in the past means that very little provision is made for strategic thinking

5 Executives are given broad terms of reference but are denied real power. The resulting uncertainties create a good deal of jostling for position

6 Executives operate individually and there is no clear control from the top. Significant things happen only through informal plotting

7 Individual appointments make no provision for decision-making but consultation is encouraged. So people meet to determine how they can best operate

8 Individual appointments are made in a company lacking a clear structure or in the process of transformation

9 The boss takes the decisions but allows subordinates free rein. Unpredictable behaviour results on the part of both the boss and other senior executives

10 People find their own level and work collectively. Communication between different levels, however, can be poor

11 Good team-building and communications facilitate the distribution of work and decision-taking

12 A social organization lacking structure, in which everyone has a say

13 The boss runs the show and people are not sure about the nature of their jobs. Anything can happen

14 People are appointed without clear terms of reference. Decision-making is subject to personalities and to intrigue

15 People are appointed without clear terms of reference but are brought into a social environment where everyone is taken into account

16 A voluntary gathering of a number of people where no one holds any authority or contributes valued experience

---

empowerment can only come about after time and thought has been put into construction of jobs and the collectivity of jobs within a work area. Here communication plays a crucial role. A great deal of benefit is gained by using a universal language on jobs with its appropriate discipline. Only in that way can one hope to design effective and mutually understood procedures.

Everyone must know what constitutes Yellow and Orange work and what part must be played by Blue and Green.

Empowering an individual and empowering a team raise very different issues. The former depends on the adequacy of an understanding between A, the manager, and B, the jobholder. If A trusts B and B knows what A wants and the tolerance limits within which to work, much can be achieved with very little formal agreement. But as empowerment is spread to encompass several people who work together, the range of possibilities rapidly mounts. Individuals can overlap in their presumed responsibilities and gaps can be created because everyone has presumed that something was not their responsibility. Essential tasks can become the focus of effort or be ignored just as easily. Making assumptions about empowerment in its wider application is full of traps.

The truth of the matter is that within a structured organization there is no such thing as self-empowerment. Nor can a group or team be totally self-empowered. Somebody – a manager, a consultant or a trained facilitator – needs to empower somebody else and the recipient needs to be a party to the process. Empowerment can only become effective when it is the end result of a semi-political process that leads to mutual agreement. In terms of work roles, empowerment necessitates an increasing level of Yellow work and Orange work at all levels. A person may be empowered or a team may be empowered in whatever combination is appropriate. There must be commitment to this overall strategy if progress is to be made. And the information generated by our pilot studies suggests a particular set of cultural conditions will be needed if the benefits of empowerment are to be reaped by the organization as a whole.

Finally, one must concede that in poorly structured organizations self-empowerment does arise. That is because empowerment does not clash with anything already there because there is not much to clash with. The empowerment gained by individuals and teams heralds the collapse of the corporate body and creates the background for the spin-off of new enterprises. Collapsing systems create new opportunities – but it is a high price to pay for progress.

THE DEVELOPING NATURE
OF TEAMWORK

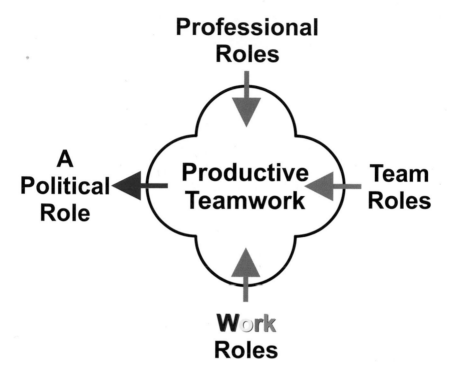

Professional Roles

A Political Role

Productive Teamwork

Team Roles

Work Roles

Figure 1: The Developing Nature of Teamwork

When new appointments are made, jobholders first interpret their jobs in terms of their professional education and training. Later jobholders discover the importance of meaningful team roles. Improved teamwork produces many benefits. Yet a well-motivated team may eventually slide towards an inward focus. In a new era a rapidly changing world is calling for an outward focus and a quicker responsiveness to new demands. It is here that the language and discipline of work roles has a part to play with its emphasis on expanding and developing jobs in a continuous process. While so gaining in strength and breadth, teamwork may nonetheless encounter new problems. Impositions placed on the team by a remotely-placed hierarchy or by the bureaucracy of the encompassing group threaten a culture clash. Progress then depends on how well the team can master a political role needed to negotiate a greater level of empowerment. Progress depends too on the likelihood of reform in the operating characteristics of the wider organization.

SIZE versus EFFICIENCY

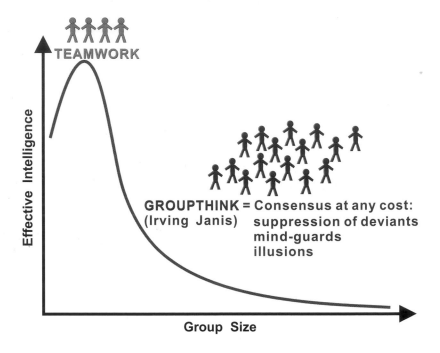

Figure 2: Size versus Efficiency

Intelligence in terms of work output can be boosted by interaction with others. But as the numbers involved increase, intelligent behaviour declines.

SIX DIFFERENCES BETWEEN A TEAM AND A GROUP

	TEAM	GROUP
SIZE	LIMITED	MEDIUM or LARGE
SELECTION	CRUCIAL	IMMATERIAL
LEADERSHIP	SHARED or ROTATING	SOLO
PERCEPTION	MUTUAL KNOWLEDGE UNDERSTANDING	FOCUS ON LEADER
STYLE	ROLE SPREAD CO-ORDINATION	CONVERGENCE CONFORMISM
SPIRIT	DYNAMIC INTERACTION	TOGETHERNESS PERSECUTION OF OPPONENTS

Figure 3: Six Differences between a Team and a Group

An exercise for Workshops has been to ask participants to distinguish between teams and groups. Many features that people see as typifying teams are present to some extent in groups. Few identified the two features at the top of the list found to have the most radical effect on collective behaviour.

WORK ROLES

Core Work

	Tasks	Responsibilities

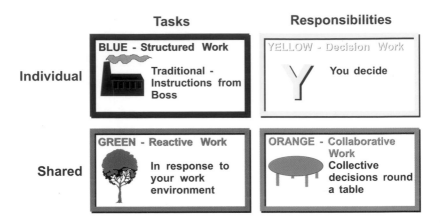

	Tasks	Responsibilities
Individual	BLUE - Structured Work — Traditional - Instructions from Boss	YELLOW - Decision Work — You decide
Shared	GREEN - Reactive Work — In response to your work environment	ORANGE - Collaborative Work — Collective decisions round a table

Additional Work

GREY - Incidental Work	WHITE - Creative / New Work	PINK - Imaginary Work
Expanding the job — The Job	Your own initiative - outside normal duties — New Ideas	Pink Elephant / Pink Panther

Figure 4: Work Roles

A visual illustration used to convey the seven colour-based elements of the work role. Emotional and political pre-associations sometimes create resistance to accepting the meanings. That problem can be overcome by emphasizing the logic underlining the choice of particular colours.

SEVEN TYPES OF PINK WORK

1	**Collecting redundant information**
	"I've received that too"
2	**Demanding information that is never used**
	"Write me a report, and by the way, I'll be away for a month"
3	**Collecting obsolete information**
	"Well, it might come in useful"
4	**Waiting for work**
	"It should have been here ages ago"
5	**Empty antics**
	"You can go through the procedures, but I know what's going to be decided anyway"
6	**Unnecessary travelling**
	"I think I'll pay them a visit anyway"
7	**Meetings**
	"After all that talk, what a waste of time"

Figure 5: Seven Types of Pink Work

Jobholders seldom find difficulty in identifying Pink Work. These usually fall into recurring categories.

MEETINGS

DESCRIPTION	IDEAL SIZE	PURPOSE	MODE OF CONDUCT
Personal discussion	2 or 3	Creating a strategy	Formless
Chance encounter	4 and under	Coming up with ideas	Leaderless
The creative team	Selected 4-5	Purposive creativity	Rotating leadership
The project team	Selected 4-6	Problem solving	Appointed project leader
The task focused group	6-8	Operational planning	Project co-ordinator
The structured group	8-12	Redirected effort	Manager led
Formal meeting	12-20	Inter-departmental meeting with fixed agenda	Best senior co-ordinator
Formal announcements	20+	Focus on new policies	Solo leader role
The conference	Any number	Professional gathering	A reputable chairperson

Figure 6: Meetings

Meetings should be designed for a purpose. Purposes are better not combined as they call for different people in different desired numbers. As a general rule, the more people present the shorter should be the meeting.

CULTURE AND DECISION-MAKING
Mode of Decision-Making

Work Culture		TOP-PERSON	SMALL CIRCLES	CONSULTATION AND CONSENSUS	OBSCURE
	PEOPLE IN STRUCTURED JOBS	Boss-run Bureaucracy 1	Senior Team with boxes underneath 2	Management by Committee 3	The Dinosaur Organization 4
	OBJECTIVES – THE REST IS UP TO INDIVIDUALS	Competitive Individualism, Fragmented Efforts 5	Competitive Cabals 6	Meetings to resolve Work Roles 7	The Formless Organization 8
	GROUP MEMBERS DISTRIBUTE WORK AMONGST THEMSELVES	Loose-cannon Management, Wasted resources 9	Layered Teamwork 10	Team Empowerment 11	The Commune 12
	NO CLEAR PATTERN	Seat-of-pants Management 13	Byzantine Management 14	The Cotton Wool Organization 15	The Leaderless Congregation 16

Figure 7: Culture and Decision-Making

The mode of decision-making was found to be less related to the work-culture than had been supposed. Some combinations of decision-making and culture are especially unrewarding and Team Empowerment is rare.

FATAL INCENTIVES

Figure 8: Fatal Incentives

Emphasis on short-term financial results may hasten the ultimate downfall of a company. This mistake is taken from a set of talks on *The seven recurring mistakes of the twentieth century in the management of people and organizations.*

[Illustration reproduced by kind permission of 'The Economist' and Satoshi Kambayashi - © The Economist, London (7 August 1999).]

TYPES OF DECISION-MAKING

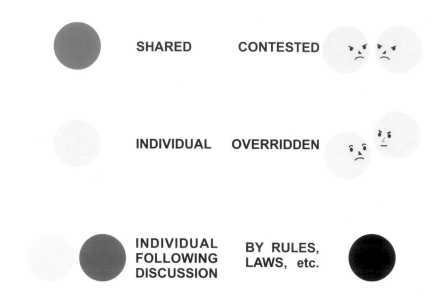

Figure 9: Types of Decision-Making

The three most effective types of decision-making can be represented by colloquialisms.

Orange signifies "We think and we decide"

Yellow signifies "I think and I decide"

Yellow and Green signifies "We discuss and I decide"

The three most commonly found forms of ineffective decision-making can be represented by the following:

Two Yellows side by side gives rise to "No, I disagree. I think we should….."

Yellow above Yellow results in "So how have you exercised your responsibility? No, I think that is a mistake. You had better……."

Blue is associated with "Well, whatever the customer may say, this is what the specification calls for."

Bad decisions arise from bad organizational practice and side-stepping good practice.

RISK versus COMPLEXITY

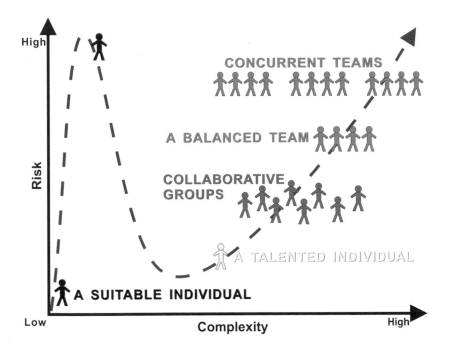

Figure 10: Risk versus Complexity

The number of people who should ideally be involved in a particular activity depends on the colour classification of the work. The colour of the work in turn is related to the seriousness of mishaps if things go wrong (risk) and the number of variables in the situation (complexity). Where everything is known about how a task is best executed, a competent individual should be assigned to the work. The risk of mistakes may be high but that is only an additional reason why the rigorous demands of Blue Work should be respected. Where more complexity is involved over-specification of the work is undesirable and it is better policy to pass responsibility over to a suitably talented person. As complexity increases further still, other people need to become involved, for they may have vital information that is lacking. Rising risk and complexity eventually makes for difficult decision-making. That becomes the point at which the composition of the team becomes critical. In very demanding decision areas there are advantages in lowering risk by setting up independent and well balanced teams operating in parallel. Their outputs are likely to put difficult issues in perspective and will facilitate ultimate decisions. This approach stands in sharpest contrast to hierarchical decision-making with its intolerance of challenge to Authority.

SNAKES AND LADDERS

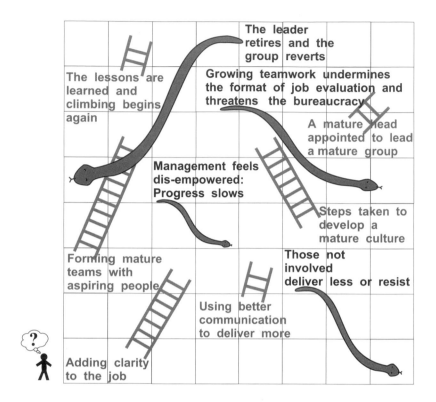

The leader retires and the group reverts

The lessons are learned and climbing begins again

Growing teamwork undermines the format of job evaluation and threatens the bureaucracy

A mature head appointed to lead a mature group

Management feels dis-empowered: Progress slows

Steps taken to develop a mature culture

Forming mature teams with aspiring people

Those not involved deliver less or resist

Using better communication to deliver more

Adding clarity to the job

Figure 11: Snakes and Ladders

Changing the way jobs are set up and managed strikes at the heart of organizations. A system is more than the sum of its parts. If one part is changed, the system fights back to recover its original shape. Progress is made up of forward and backward steps. Progress would be faster should the system be tackled as a whole from the outset.

Chapter

8

Rewards and remuneration

In previous pages I have described the four distinct types of work activity that can underlie the construction of any job. These variable components of a job allow greater control over how a job is executed. Yet this change in approach complicates the relationship between a given work content and a particular form of remuneration. How then in general does the theory and practice of work roles impinge on payment systems?

We know the question is bound to arise because pilot projects soon run into problems once changes made to jobs affect the way jobholders are paid or expect to be paid. Many a manager would prefer to retain a job in its original form, so sacrificing the benefits on offer from expansion or improvement, rather than face up to the pressure to review the level of remuneration that a revised job carries. Such is the dilemma that public and private sector organizations face when they become locked into formal job evaluation. An astute jobholder, sometimes assisted by trade union backing, will be quick to point out that the expanded job entails new responsibilities that need to be rewarded. There is no easy answer to that undeniable claim other than to pay out more money or to recruit another person to carry out the extra work. In other words, improving the job is treated as an exceptional activity. It in no way forms part of a jobholder's normal duties. That is the current position in many large companies.

The question now to be considered is whether we should find a new starting-point. Before one can begin, a further re-examination of current practice is called for. As a first step, and in order to understand it better, the administration of job evaluation needs to be put under the spotlight. What work role does it entail? One must inevitably conclude that its essence in a bureaucracy is Blue work. The implicit theme is that the system is so well thought out, so comprehensive and so precise, that two well-trained people will inevitably arrive at the same quantitative conclusion about what a job is worth. That is what is supposed to put the subject beyond controversy. Turning the number of points collected into remuneration for the job then becomes no more than a mechanical operation. In other words, discretion is taken away from managers and transferred to job evaluation technicians.

Given that job evaluation is a Blue work procedure, designed to provide a basis for payment differentials, the question now arises as to its most appropriate application. Job evaluation aims to establish the basic rate for the job. But, additionally, its highly structured character lends itself to performance-related pay. The most favoured application seems to be other Blue work. Wherever Blue work arises, how the job is to be performed can be set out precisely. There is total clarity about the nature of the outputs and these will vary according to skill and effort. The most long-standing instances of performance-related pay apply significantly to repetitive manual operations where the traditional system of payment has been piecework. An X number of pieces leads to a Y amount of money. $2X$ equals $2Y$, $3X$ equals $3Y$ and so forth. If one form of Blue work is more arduous than another, or carried out under difficult conditions, that will be taken care of by job evaluation under 'Conditions' and will earn extra points. In that way differentials are built up. So different manual operations will carry different standard starting rates and there is a mathematical relationship between the pay for the basic job and anything that is achieved above the basic level of expectation. The format is relatively simple.

Now consider the type of work to which job evaluation is least applicable. Here one must nominate Green work. How the work is done depends on the people, the clients and the situation. Social skills, diplomacy, the willingness to provide support and help to others are all abstract concepts that do not lend themselves to easy measurement. The social skills of an able receptionist or an ill-paid nurse operating in the field of mental health may easily be the equal of someone negotiating a big business deal. The skill demands of Green work can hardly form the basis of an easily administered payment system.

In the case of Orange work the demands and output of a team can also be abstract in nature and so too defy easy evaluation. A new product development team may design a brilliant new product; but its success or failure will depend on other initiatives within the company. Orange work is not a self-standing operation but a contributor to the larger whole. Its outputs will be unique and not comparable in any objective sense with other outputs. Nor would it make much sense to consider the demands of Orange work as a basis for payment. Capricious factors may account for any invitation to join strategic or policy-making teams. If such invitations were to qualify for points under job evaluation, there would no doubt be a general rush for executives to find tables around which they might confer! Nor does the social basis of Orange work credibly lend itself to the application of individual performance-related pay.

Finally, one turns to Yellow work. Here the case for job evaluation and individual performance-related pay is far more strongly established. The concept of Yellow work is close to that of Management by Objectives. The size of the Yellow work is indicated through job evaluation under 'Responsibilities'. However, the term is used in a different sense from the way in which it is used in the language of work roles. In the language of job evaluation, the term Responsibilities covers People, Financial Resources and Physical Resources. The greater the span of control, the more staff come under a manager, the bigger the budget over which the manager has financial discretion, and the more costly the capital invested in physical resources, the more remunerative the job becomes. No doubt that is one of the reasons why some middle managers are keen to build up their empires and are reluctant to economize or slim down in the resources they utilize. So job evaluation, with its focus on inputs rather than outputs, rewards waste and extravagance. Its mode of operation increases the likelihood of getting less out of the job!

Performance-related pay, in contrast, places its focus on the output of the job. Such a system has particular attractions for top managers. The higher the managerial rank the easier it becomes to express performance in financial terms. Not only does it commend itself for its ease of application but it also operates as a strong motivational force. The generally accepted method is to turn manufacturing or operating units into profit centres. The person in charge is regarded as the generator of the profit. On the face of it, the incentive should produce the desired corporate results.

However, some long-term American research generated in the Harvard Business School and quoted in *The Economist* (7 August 1999) presents a different picture and accords with what I have found in the UK. Where managers have been awarded generous share options linked to the profitability of the company, long-term profitability has been found to fall in comparison with companies where such schemes are absent. The explanation is that top managers, often near the age of retirement, are well placed to manipulate the profits of a company in order to provide impressive short-term results. Selling fixed assets, reducing or revaluing stocks and curtailing research and development are well-established devices for achieving that aim. Managers are then well placed to cash in their shares and buy retirement annuities. The strong incentive produces the opposite of what might be desired in the long term. Adopting such a formula can be a fatal move if the company's real interests are taken to heart (see Figure 8).

Performance-related pay is being applied increasingly to middle managers as well as top managers. After all, middle managers undertake a great deal of Yellow work and they are often in the real driving seat. The favoured emphasis is often on some easily measured indicator of financial performance. Yet this too can lead in unexpected and unwelcome directions. For example, one leading high street bank devised a scheme for rewarding bank managers according to the amount of new business transacted. It so happens that much of what counts as new business is *lending*. The lending rate shot up accordingly – but so too did bad debts!

Performance-related pay has its roots in the widespread assumption that people will only do their jobs well if they are offered the prospect of more money. An alternative view is that most people, if they like their job and are properly selected, will wish to do their jobs well anyway. In that case the emphasis will shift to finding an appropriate level of remuneration for the job itself. That is why formal job evaluation receives so much attention in the field of public service.

However, the question now is whether the right sort of approach is being adopted in the light of the changing nature of jobs. The old compartmentalized descriptions of jobs have begun to lose their relevance to the modern world. Jobs are increasingly becoming accretions: they are built up in serial layers of work activity in a continuous process where there are no hard and fast boundaries. All these work activities are open to classification according to the notion of work roles. However, to use these inputs to serve or replace the conventional yardsticks that underlie job evaluation is hardly feasible. Two of these roles (Green and Orange) cannot easily be assimilated into the system for the reasons that have been given above. It is debatable as to whether Blue and Yellow can be combined in a meaningful way that jobholders could readily follow. But, in any case, if two of the four essential work roles were left out of account, the overall result would be a distortion. It would mean that jobs were being forced into a conceptual procrustean bed in order to achieve an objective that can possibly be reached more simply by other means.

That susceptibility to distort the direction of effort already noted with Yellow work has its parallel in the case of Blue work. This is the other area to which individual incentives are often applied and are prone to bring about damage. In the case of Blue work the usual emphasis on productivity entails the risk of sacrificing quality for quantity. As a result, the customer may suffer along with the reputation of the company or the service. But that is not the only problem. The link of pay with quantity presumes that effort and skill are correlated with output. The reality is that defective raw materials and delays in delivery often upset the link between diligence and performance. As far as Blue work is concerned, anomalies in the reward system commonly undermine good industrial relations and lower morale.

An overview is now needed on how performance-related pay is working out at the present time. On the face of it, the case for the proposition sounds reasonable enough. It offers an incentive to perform well and carries with it the sense of justice – those who work well or hard should benefit from their labours. But there is more to it than that. The ultimate test is what effect it has not only on particular jobholders but on other workers as well as on materials and products.

Performance-related income, akin to performance-related pay, is regrettably being applied on somewhat arbitrary criteria to whole organizations. Here the effects are worth noting as they operate in the public sector. Take the National Heath Service. Successive governments have attempted to manipulate its performance through allocating or withholding expenditure: here are some recorded examples. One of the criteria selected comprised the number of patients treated in hospitals and the cost of treatment (basing this on a standard cost of an occupied bed). Spectacular improvements were soon claimed by higher authorities: there was a rise in the number of patients treated and bed occupancy showed a greater rate of through-put – that is to say, beds were occupied for shorter periods. Upon closer examination, it transpired that the same patients were being readmitted after being prematurely discharged from their beds. In their re-entry they were being counted as different patients. Premature discharge from hospital can ultimately be registered as a form of efficiency, when in fact it is the reverse.

How long patients were obliged to wait in Outpatient Departments became another focus of attention. Here again ingenuity knew no bounds. Some hospitals created what became known as a *hostess nurse*. The patient would be seen and interviewed in a pleasant way but with the real intention of reducing the recorded waiting-time. Patients would of course be no nearer treatment – but more Brownie points would be gained. Government has developed a close interest in waiting lists, an aspect of medical efficiency which readily lends itself to examination by non-professionals. Hospitals are threatened with financial penalties if given waiting times are exceeded. A recent case reported to me illustrates how this issue is being handled. An acquaintance had been waiting for some months for an operation to a hand. To his surprise, the hospital reported that they were glad to say that he could now be put on the *official* waiting list. Apparently there were two waiting lists – one where the records were available to government and another that reflected reality.

An immediate reaction might be to cast blame on the hospitals concerned and their readiness to engage in misinformation. What should one make of their tendency to engage in evasive procedures in response to top-down impositions? Does it mean they are shirking their responsibilities? I think not. Many professionals, faced with a conflict situation, consider that their prime responsibility lies towards patients rather than to government. It may be argued that government is endeavouring to transfer responsibility to hospitals that have hitherto been acting fecklessly. But I do not think that argument can hold. A responsibility needs to be a contract freely entered into by two parties. A so-called responsibility *imposed* by a superior level in a hierarchy becomes in effect a task. Yet, how can that task be classified? It is certainly not Blue work, for it does not involve precision in mode of operation; nor is it Green work, since it does not entail responsiveness to the realities of the situation. This type of imposed task is clearly conceived by the recipients of this top-down imposition as Pink work. So a silly task results in a silly answer.

Expenditure on education has become subject to similar forces. Schools that produce good examination results, based on the grades received, gain extra resources. The effect has been to hold back pupils from taking exams where the average grade might be lowered. Another restrictive effect has been to limit the number of subjects that a pupil may take in an examination. Here the idea has been to eliminate the poorer grades presumed to accompany a more extended set of subjects. The distorting effect of particular measurements is of course nothing new in the field of education. The mindless drilling of pupils in Victorian schools was, according to Mathew Arnold, the fault of the exam system. Retention was what mattered; pupils would thus learn by heart but understand little. Mindless recapitulation of knowledge is still a feature of education in many underdeveloped parts of the world and a likely handicap to economic development.

As performance-related pay moves down from the corporate body to the individual worker, similar and predictable distortions in performance occur. In Jobcentres staff are judged by the number of placements they make. Investigations have shown that some staff fiddle the figures so as to inflate the number of placements. An unemployed person may be sent for a job interview and the outcome presumed without adequate confirmation. An allied area, now giving rise to suspicion, arises from the incentive to perform on the part of the police. Arrests and convictions provide criteria for promotion. The planting of incriminating evidence on suspects has become a worrying feature of miscarriages of justice. Unwanted knock-on effects are also to be observed in another field. The individual effectiveness of teachers is now being judged by the examination grades their pupils obtain. One troubling outcome of this practice is that random tests of teachers by inspectors have shown that some teachers have opened the envelopes containing the exam papers early and coached their pupils through the questions.

Although illegalities will naturally excite public attention and are not to be condoned, there are other less prominent ways in which the top-down evaluation of performance undermines a public service. The typical case is that of traffic wardens. The number of tickets issued has been seized on by some local authorities as an easy way of comparing the effectiveness of one traffic warden with another. The effect, however, in the competition for advancement can be to remove discretion on the part of the traffic warden as to why a vehicle is temporarily parked where it is. A valued community service cannot easily be built on bad public relations.

All these examples tell a similar story. That story is that certain types of remuneration system can have an undesired effect on the way in which people perform in their work roles. The major objections to job evaluation and to performance-related pay are that, jointly, they undermine teamwork, distort output and create anomalies, so generating resentment and lowering morale.

Yet the concept of job evaluation appeals for its apparent rationality. If job evaluation did not exist, it would beg to be invented. Does it not seem fair that those who work hard, have superior skills or toil under difficult conditions should earn more than others in less demanding jobs? It would be difficult for anyone to disagree. Job evaluation can also serve several purposes, not only providing a framework for differentials but also a starting-point for formulating strategies for recruitment. What must be questioned, however, is whether a fixed and comprehensive system can serve for all these various purposes.

The formal approach of job evaluation provides one strategy for managing remuneration. If that strategy should be rejected for some of the reasons given above, what other options are available? One approach is to reject formalities and to rely on person-based judgements. The choice here lies between the singular or the plural. In other words, remuneration issues can be treated as fit for either individual Yellow work or collective Orange work. Under the theory of work roles these constitute the two prime modes of decision-making. Yellow work is the normal approach in small firms run by an owner–manager. There is no bureaucracy, so the owner–manager is unfettered and can take a decision on how much a new employee should be paid. Should any difficulty arise, negotiations can take place on the spot. Yellow work under such conditions can be recommended for its delightful simplicity.

In a larger organization more complications arise. How much one person is paid can have repercussions on others. People will be alerted towards anomalies. They will watch for examples of what they consider unfairness or for discrepancies between what management declares and what actually happens. Ideally, justice should be done. And it is equally important that justice should be perceived to be done. Such a potentially controversial area is the ideal field for Orange work. A well-balanced team will be invited to address particular cases. For political reasons it may be deemed advisable to change the composition of the team from time to time and even to bring in suitable members from different levels of the organization. Here certain issues need to be looked at closely. How can such teams be kept free from vested interests in practice? Should team members be restricted from presiding over the pay of close colleagues? Can the equality of authority be preserved among team members drawn from different levels? These and similar issues need to be discussed and an under-standing reached before new mechanisms for pay determination are put into operation. The team may change from time to time and it is desirable that it should. But one factor will always stay constant: responsibility for any verdict reached will be shared by the team members, so no particular member will be exposed. Each verdict will be an outcome of 'all factors considered' and, unlike job evaluation, will not depend solely on a formula.

The need for Orange work is an acknowledgement that complex issues are involved and these are best handled by thought and discussion. Yet sight should never be lost of the underlying position. The price of a salary, like any other commodity, is ultimately set by the market. If people feel they are under-paid, they will leave. If a salary on offer compares well with what is available elsewhere, there will be an ample supply of applicants. Yet while supply and demand may form basic guidelines they cannot serve as the universal means of determining salary differentials. Inevitably, many jobs indigenous to a firm will not be comparable with any recognized job in the labour market. Yet the sense of equity must still prevail. How does that job compare with some benchmark job where the appropriate level of remuneration is more easily established? Only the Orange Team is in a position to make that decision. Difficult though that decision may be, it will be treated with respect to the extent that members of the Orange Team are themselves respected.

To sum up, I believe that the institutionalization of job evaluation in large organizations to cover every job is inadvisable. It consumes vast amounts of time and paperwork, raises heightened expectations on equity and stokes up dissatisfaction when those expectations are not met. More important still, it creates rigidity in the way in which jobs operate and inhibits their development.

Yet the establishment of fair differentials is generally considered important. Here it can be useful for benchmark jobs to be selected by managers as reference points. These may be few in number but are useful as guidelines, especially where jobs operate on boundaries between departments or encompass rare skills in short supply. Here the suggested approach is Orange work. The team selected to perform this work needs to be chosen with political care and there is no reason why a shortened form of job evaluation should not be used. What differs about this recommendation is that it should be related to the occasional (significant) job and that it should not become part of a general routine.

Motivation at the workplace is not simply about money. Financial remuneration should always be adequate to retain valued employees and be consistent with policies and promises. Most people will accept what they believe to be a fair rate for the job and after that other forms of reward and fulfilment are sought. We know from survey and research literature that one of the most highly regarded rewards is *recognition*. People need others to take an interest in what they are doing and to give credit when a job is well done. Here the work-role feedback system provides the information upon which such judgements can be made. Appreciation is a form of private recognition. Public recognition can be even more motivating, especially where it is associated with prize giving. Prizes associated with work roles are particularly suitable for Teamwork and Job Growth (the latter awarded to a jobholder who has added most value to a job). Such awards are found to excite congratulations from others rather than resentment. The reason would appear to be linked with expectations. Few people expect to receive a prize, but many expect to receive their due bonus. What is expected and not received causes despondency bordering on despair. What is not expected but given comes as a welcome surprise. I believe that the term *awards* should be confined to benefits given without being promised. *Rewards*, on the other hand, refer to benefits both promised and conferred. In a rapidly changing world, systems that boldly promise rewards invite the hand of Nemesis. But awards, retrospectively given, are safer and will always be at hand to suit any situation.

Time-off, treats and subsidized parties offer a variety of awards, in addition to remuneration, for raising morale at the workplace. Yet the features of work that most appeal often depend on intrinsic rather than extrinsic factors. The most contented jobholders are usually working in tune with their natural team roles and work roles and in fields that create opportunities for their aptitudes and expressed interests. That is the broad area to which effective managers need to direct their attention.

9

Adding value to the job

When a manager spells out the specific demands of a job, the employee is constrained to act within its limits. It would be inviting to the ambitious and the creative to be told 'I want you to come into this job and see what you can make of it', but only in the very senior reaches of management are jobs normally given such elastic boundaries. Even in the case of the core work, itself the starting-point for the application of work roles, it is rare to find that the average jobholder will depart very far from what he or she is required to do. It is seldom a matter of laziness or lack of initiative. There are definite hazards facing employees who cheerily wander over their job boundaries. One illustration is the complaints one hears about newly appointed graduates who disregard protocol or who 'poke their nose into other people's business'. What is usually meant is that they have encroached, often innocently, into some incumbent's closely guarded territory. Conversely, the virtues of circumspection are much appreciated. Those with limited abilities, who never put a foot wrong in their dealings with other people and other departments, often earn themselves a secure position.

To expand the boundaries of a job requires a licence. In other words, the jobholder needs to be told specifically that an extension of the core work is both permissible and even desirable. When our pilot studies into the use of work roles began, we soon noted the discrepancy between what a manager thought a jobholder did, or should do, and what a jobholder actually did. A typical jobholder would disclose to us, somewhat diffidently, why something that he or she was supposed to do had been dropped and some other action put in its place. The reasons for the variation might be sound but the jobholder would be very reluctant to communicate the reality to the manager. Hence the communication system between manager and jobholder was found to be decidedly one-sided. It was a case of a great deal of traffic from the top down but very little in the opposite direction. There were secrets to which the manager would not be privy.

In a well-disciplined company it is difficult to excite interest in Pink work in the early stages. Efficient companies don't admit to having any Pink work. Should the subject be raised, it can become a source of embarrassment. The implication is that the jobholder is at fault in using time badly. That position has of course to be corrected. It is not the jobholder who is wasting time, it is the jobholder's time that is being wasted. The difference may sound subtle in terms of the spoken word, but the two conditions are far apart. In the first case the jobholder is the culprit, in the latter, the victim.

Reactions are altogether more positive when a miscellaneous assembly of people is introduced to Pink work. Defensiveness vanishes. People speak freely. As we noted earlier, the whole subject becomes fun. There is nothing more calculated to generate hilarity than exposing the mistakes and absurdities of others or of the system itself. That same atmosphere needs to be cultivated back in the workplace. It may be politically difficult but it can be done. It will happen once the citing of Pink work is seen as a valued service. For that to happen a spirit of openness needs to be cultivated. Examples can be quoted of how the identification of Pink work has led to its elimination. Finding Pink work opens the road to progress.

While the citing of Pink work adds value to a job by what might be described as the negation of negation, in practice it is not the prime source of improvement. Of the three work roles that jobholders add to the job, Grey work is the one most commonly encountered. Grey work refers to that area that surrounds the core of the job and is often blurred and indistinct. A jobholder is not officially obliged to undertake some marginal activity unless it forms a specified part of the job. Tasks that are necessary but unglamorous are scarcely likely to be presented to job applicants. Nevertheless assumptions are made. Someone has to fetch materials, cope with contingencies, post the mail, bring in refreshments or help in a variety of other ways. A labourer or a junior may be assigned to these ancillary duties. But the greater likelihood is that a manager will expect jobholders to undertake any ancillary work that falls in their vicinity. Here the willingness of employees to make themselves useful over and above their official duties is a highly valued asset. This quality of an extra dimension of employability is highly valued by managers, just as it is by work associates. There is always work to be done that could not be anticipated and its burden is bound to fall on someone. It is a load that will be lightened by those who anticipate what may go wrong and are ready to take the appropriate action.

However, anticipation is not the complete answer. Recording Grey work enables an overview to be taken of miscellaneous activities. What are they? Can they be treated in an organized way? Can Grey work be diverted from a jobholder whose talents can be employed to better effect? An under-investment in job-planning is sure to inflate the amount of Grey work. Conversely, when more thought is given to planning, aided by a supply of good information, key personnel will stand a better chance of using their available time more productively.

The third type of work role that adds to the value of a job is White work. White is the colour of a blank sheet of paper. With White work it is as though one is starting with nothing. A flash of insight tells the jobholder, 'There is a better way of doing this.' Here it is important in the construction of a job that the jobholder is empowered to initiate any improvement that falls within the jobholder's domain. Yet that licence cannot be entirely open-ended. Rather it is better conceived as provisional. Information should be fed back to the manager that White work has been introduced. The subject is now on the agenda for further consideration. The response may be 'Yes, let's go on doing it that way.' Alternatively, 'Yes, that could be a solution but it might be better tackled by ...'. More negatively, 'No, we could run into problems here if we take that approach.'

Adding value to a job from the inside is impossible in the case of jobs with fixed boundaries. If improvements are to be made, they will come about only through the intervention of an outsider. A sharp contrast arises when flexible jobs are set up on the basis of the four core roles, but enabling the jobholder to expand the job through the avenue of the Pink, the Grey and the White. Here one can cite ways in which static jobs have suddenly changed. For example, in manufacturing industry a long-tolerated level of scrap and waste has been suddenly reduced. In hi-tech offices administrators who received routine telephone calls and enquiries have taken an interest in finding customers and promoting sales. Others who have been handling problems relating to the products and services of suppliers have taken it upon themselves to read the Yellow Pages telephone directory and investigate other possible suppliers. Professionals have been protected from unjustified demands on their time by the initiatives of ancillary staff, especially in dealing with calls. In one insurance company clerical staff replaced unsatisfactory standard letters with a new range of recommended responses for dealing with enquiries and complaints. In one hospital where technical medical staff were in short supply the staff themselves found a means of reducing their regulation number by off-loading some of their less essential work on to semi-skilled personnel who could be more easily recruited. Proposals to reduce manning levels along such lines are very unlikely to be initiated by jobholders in highly structured jobs. The reason is clear whenever people have well-defined job descriptions: once the need for some additional work is identified, there is no means of coping within existing resources. That is why staff will be pressing 'for more help'. A contrasting situation arises when the emphasis is on creating flexible jobs. The need to identify new needs and respond to them now becomes a challenge. People say, 'We can cope. We don't need to bring in anyone.' Such is the spirit when jobholders feel they have become team players. They want to retain the existing team. Outsiders can be treated with reservation as intruders who could spoil the current team atmosphere.

The economic benefits of adding value to the job are not easily brought about, for they are the consequence of taking a number of steps in a particular order and often by one step at a time. The first step is for tasks and responsibilities within the core work to be laid out with greater clarity than ever before. That is an important move in its own right and is usually received with equanimity or even approval. People like to know what they are responsible for and where the limit ends. On the other hand, it is difficult to engage people's commitment fully with any process that is entirely top-down. At the best they can only be willing recipients of whatever briefings they are given, even if an area of personal discretion is sanctioned, so allowing them to escape from incarceration in their core roles. However, phase two ushers in a very different mood based on a new social situation. There is a certain spirit of adventure about breaking out from the periphery of a job and extending its frontiers. People become more motivated once they feel the job is something they are capable of influencing and bringing under their own control. The opportunity to affect the 'colour' of a job and to extend the range of colours that a job encompasses enables a job to become more multidimensional and less monolithic. We have always found that this extension of the job creates a sense of excitement and fulfilment.

Ironically, the economic benefits that accrue from this advance usually go more to the organization than to the jobholder. Under a conventional form of job evaluation the extension of the frontiers of the job would call for more pay. But such a claim is out of line with the notion and philosophy of work roles. It is a tenet of this approach that every job can and should have opportunities for growth. In short, expanding the job should be part of normal jobholder behaviour. Yet while this latter situation gives a huge boost to the morale of jobholders, managers have sometimes acted strangely. The supposed beneficiaries of progress often betray a measure of indifference. Perhaps it is the loss of complete control that some managers find hard to bear.

There are in fact two routes to improvement and innovation. One is to channel ideas from above and to introduce them with the authority of top management. Yet often the remoteness of foreign ideas from the scene of application weakens their soundness and applicability. Whatever their merits, it is likely that plans introduced from on high will override any local criticisms. That is because those who have to put them to the test are the recipients of instructions and not the arbiters. They may be situated at the operational level but they are not in the driving seat. Or, if they are, the controls are set at automatic pilot: any course that has been pre-arranged will run to wherever destiny beckons.

There is, however, this second road to progress, which is to stimulate improvements that can spring from below. These stimulated originators may be schooled in pragmatism rather than theory. This may be a limitation but it is not a problem. They have a mission to make a success of change, because their jobs and their personal identities are closely bound up together. They will have a commitment to make any initiative they put forward successful. They are in the position to do so because they occupy the driving seat.

Of these two roads to progress, I place more trust in the latter because it is a process and one that is in line with good cybernetic principles. The flow of communication from manager to job-holder and back to manager, where each has an equally valuable but distinctive part to play, makes for a continuous communication link. Such a process is sure in the long run to yield superior results from changes imposed from on high. When authority rules, people will carry out whatever is ordained, even if they are the first to see minor setbacks or even impending disaster.

10

Feedback and networking

As soon as a job is laid down in the modern world, it changes. Sometimes those changes are no more than oscillations that occur at the fringes of the core work. But often changes have a more permanent significance, known only to those who are close to the job itself. That is what emerged from our pilot trials with work roles. We had devised the use of colour as a means of setting up a job that would be more meaningful to jobholders than current job descriptions. Jobholders would be clearer about their responsibilities and about the division between personal work and shared work. So, after close consultation with the manager, the job would be set up in the new intended way. We then set about seeing what really happened.

A job, we were to learn, seldom seemed to work out exactly as it had been designed for a number of reasons. It usually transpired that the jobholder knew more about the reality of the job than the manager who set it up in the first place and to whom the jobholder was accountable. Some items might turn out to be obsolete or could be tackled differently from the way originally conceived. Other work that needed to be done would be missed by anyone tamely keeping to the typical job description. A system that allows someone to do what is needed is far more productive than one that insists on keeping to what has been laid down. The job might fail to work out as planned, sometimes for reasons to do with the job itself and sometimes to do with the person in the job. The jobholder could be averse to certain work generally considered essential. Of some people, it may be said, they are too busy to engage in the tasks they dislike. That could create a serious situation, even one that could be disastrous. On the other hand, enterprising jobholders can find a way round the problem: they will often swap a task with a fellow worker. Given the right sort of work culture, jobholders help each other out. And so the frontiers of the job can change. In the end the manager does not quite know what is happening.

It therefore seemed an essential step to provide feedback to the manager, the more especially in organizations where the flatness of the reporting structure meant that the manager risked getting out of touch. At first, the way in which we generated that feedback was cumbersome and time-consuming. We had made a saving in paperwork in setting up the job only for it to become inflated again when generating the desired feedback. As a remedial measure, my colleague, Barrie Watson, ingeniously borrowed a software program which went some way to reducing the workload. But in the end there was no other option: we needed software designed for the purpose. Without appropriate software we reckoned we would be frustrated in our aim to set up flexible jobs that could both guarantee that essential work was accomplished and offer room for job expansion.

The need for software here had its analogy with team roles. Team roles are useful concepts in themselves in that they describe what each person can offer in an idiosyncratic way to the working group. But teamwork is not only about a team, it is also about work. How do the valued attributes that a person brings to the team relate to the work that is done within the team? How do the members relate to each other in any joint undertaking? How well is the team balanced for the nature of the assignment it is to undertake?

Here again one needed feedback. Without it team roles could become another stereotype, replacing the existing stereotype of job titles. Our software *Interplace* started with DOS, underwent many improvements, and ended up as a sophisticated system in Windows. Amongst its many functions, those with self-knowledge about team roles could modify their views according to how they were perceived by others; at the same time both they and their managers could pinpoint the jobs for which their team-role profiles made them most suitable.

Software facilitates feedback. But the software itself needs to be facilitated at the human level. One can understand why unsupported feedback does not operate adequately in most job situations. When someone is given a job by a manager, he or she will not say, 'I don't think I can tackle a job in this way. I would prefer it to be set up like that.' The response from anybody who wants a job, or to retain an existing job, will be, 'Yes, I think I can do it.' So too, when a manager asks, 'How is the job going?' the response will not be, 'I think my time could be better employed. Some of the things I am expected to do are pointless for such and such a reason.' The response is more likely to be, 'Fine'.

The reasons for the failures of human feedback at the human level have much to do with relative status. The manager does not expect to be challenged or questioned by a jobholder. Nor would the jobholder be likely to accept any such opportunity if given. However, the presence of a facilitator was found to change the situation and to improve the effectiveness of the communication link. This innovation could be explained to both parties in terms that could be seen as advantageous to each. To the manager one could say, 'This system will tell you how the job is working out.' To the jobholder one could say, 'This gives a chance to exercise some control over your job boundaries and will give you the opportunity to grow in the job.' Both statements are true but they are not of equal importance to the respective parties.

Human feedback played the major part in making the whole system both acceptable and functional. During the pilot trials I was working with two skilful and experienced trainers, Barrie Watson in the UK and Thomas Ekbom in Sweden. With the longer-term goal of spreading the message, we did not intend to make the whole system revolve round us personally. Others needed to be trained as facilitators. Accordingly we ran facilitator training courses, which were mainly attended by designated participants from particular companies. If, however, we imagined that we had done all that was necessary in order to start a new system of job management rolling, we were to be disappointed.

The facilitators were to experience two blockages to their progress. The first related to opposition from the Establishment. Too many people within the organization have entrenched interest in the preservation of existing procedures. Change is not always welcome. Facilitators, acting as individuals, found themselves politically isolated and personally exposed. A further difficulty presented a more immediate barrier to progress. The facilitators did not leave our course with the appropriate software, as it was not yet ready. That meant they lacked the user-friendly tools that would have given their work immediate credibility. In retrospect, we now realize that we launched our courses prematurely. They fulfilled a basic educational need, which may be of long-term benefit. But they failed to get new projects started, as we had hoped. And so we had to revise our strategy. We had to invest more heavily in the technology of the new software and we had to advocate and cultivate a networking culture in which these new advances could take place. If feedback is to operate to advantage in industry and the public services, the means of delivery have to be more widely spread. Laptop computers have a vast potential for revolutionizing the way we work. The phenomenal growth in their memory systems, their extensive networking possibilities, and the ever-widening use of laptop computers among the general population mean that a vast amount of information, relevant to performance at work, could soon be at the fingertips of jobholders. At least that is the theory. The question is, will it happen?

If it does, it will truly constitute a revolution. The current reality is that the majority of employees who earn their living in large organizations occupy diminutive positions at the foothills of a hierarchy where their access to information is severely restricted. The bureaucracies that hierarchies spawn keep a close control over information flow. Information is there, almost entirely, for purposes of Blue work. It is not there to help a jobholder to make a decision; it is there to tell a worker what decision must be made. Communication is top-down. And if any additional information is being passed on, it falls within the context of Mr Big handing out scraps to the massed 'Blues'. There is no down-up process, nor does it operate even from side to side. In fact, it is not a communication system at all in the true sense of the term. It predominantly deals with the downwards flow of information. Admittedly, there are exceptions and occasionally organizations value the more general spread of information. Such information, it must be conceded, does not constitute Blue work. In fact, it is unrelated to any colour: it is no more than information-noise. A large amount of information, that has no relevance to any action that could be taken by the recipient of that information, is harmless, for it poses no threat to authority. The overall position then is that the workers are seldom told about anything that really matters to them. The lower the position in the hierarchy, the less informed people become. All this is under-standable because under traditional practice the workers are not supposed to take decisions.

Now let us consider the converse situation. Let us replace workers with jobholders. That will entail a consequential reduc-tion in Blue work and a growth in Yellow and Orange work. Jobholders will now need to make decisions and will be held accountable for the decisions they make. To make good decisions they will need information. The laptop computer now comes into its own. However, the laptop computer has yet to make its wider mark in industry, at present being largely confined to the independently operating professional and executive classes. The unhesitating exceptions are the companies that pride themselves on being at the forefront of technology. There, computer-literate project leaders and team leaders are ever ready to use the tools of their trade. Project leaders surf around the Internet and are very prone to pick up information. There is a saying that to learn a secret you must tell a secret. How much do they give away in exchange? We do not know and nor do their superiors know. But there is no doubt that the computer-literate classes are commu-nicating with each other in a way that impinges in a fundamental way on the exercise of their work roles. In terms of their behaviour they are acting as though they have been given Yellow work. They have interpreted their job as being accountable for the results that the project was set up to accomplish and so will engage in whatever actions are necessary in order to achieve the desired outcome.

In our own field of promoting the effective use of team roles, team leaders have used our software *Interplace* in order to re-balance teams, once one team member has left, and to fill vacancies by searching for the best profile from within a large company database in order to invite an appropriate application. Such procedures can be in accord with a company's personnel policy or they can be acting outside it. My impression is that the unofficial is more usual than the official. For one thing, the law acts as an obstruction by hedging the use of personnel data with restrictions. The more serious operating problem is that personnel policies have been framed for delivery in a pre-computer-literate age and are supervised by senior executives who are not only computer-phobes but have a vested interest in the maintenance of the hierarchical bureaucracy.

We must now recognize that in most large organizations of the present era there are two classes jockeying for position in the control of organization. There are the Networkers and their opponents, the representatives of the hierarchical bureaucracy, whom we will call the HBs. The HBs hold the levers of power since they are the lackeys of the Top. The HBs can kill the Networkers in any head-to-head encounter. On the other hand, there is quite a lot going for the Networkers. They are operating a system unknown to the HBs, whereas they themselves are only too aware of the practices and traditions of the HBs. In respect of mutual knowledge, one side is definitely better equipped than the other. However, such is the divergence between the functioning characteristics of the two sides that they may have little common ground on which to meet. In other words, two systems may co-exist and overcome the likelihood of conflict by mutual avoidance. The Networkers have one final advantage over the HBs in that they are part of a rising trend, whereas the HBs may already have reached the zenith of their influence.

In the great majority of organizations the HBs are at present dominant. The Networkers lack the confidence and the necessary mandate to advance their position. The prospects of each party depend on the culture of the organization. Yet where the Networkers have gained the ascendancy, theirs is a very strong competitive position. That must be the general explanation of how it is that Microsoft, a classic example of a Networking company, knocked that solid HB company, IBM, off its perch as the world's largest. But that setback ultimately brought about a transformation of IBM itself. Networking vastly increases the scope of accomplishment. But Networking is not just about technology; it is about how jobs are constructed and operate. It is about the very nature of organization.

Chapter
11

Decision-making and the mature team

Well-constructed and well-balanced teams have a good chance of succeeding in the modern world. But success is not ensured, however well the team functions. A common problem lies with the environment of the team. The team may be mature but the organization may not be. Hierarchies run organizations. They tolerate teams but are loath to see teams as alternatives to hierarchical decision-making, as the evidence cited in Chapter 7 indicates. Close analysis shows that, whatever utterances may be made to the contrary, hierarchies are prone to furnish teams with tasks rather than with real responsibilities. Here teams compare unfavourably in this respect with committees. Committees are commonly overloaded with members, they are often presented with matters of marginal or no interest to some of those present, they overrun the time-slot envisaged when the agenda was formed and invitations despatched, they are profligate wasters of time. Yet that is where key and binding decisions will be made. How is it then that committees, so operationally ineffective in many instances, carry more guns than effective teams in terms of weight and influence?

In my experience the reason is simple. Senior people sit on committees. Their presence ensures empowerment. Others, in more lowly positions, who seize on any invitation to join committees, are there as a concession and are therefore under an obligation. They find favour by associating with the mighty and endorsing whatever decisions their seniors make. So the democratic form of committees can be illusory in practice. The votes of the lowly will scarcely outweigh those of high rank. In practice the decisive element in decision-making is person-power rather than the numerical count of hands, and the larger the committee the more this principle holds.

So-called teams, without the presence of power-brokers, are usually set up by hierarchies with a limited purpose in view. They are usually there to look into issues; to generate information or recommendations for others to act on. However, should a senior person be included in the party, the team then risks not becoming a team. Its characteristics will be that of a led group. With such forces ranged so heavily against the prospects for teams, how can the situation be retrieved?

It is here that work roles come into play. Every team that embarks on a mission is entitled to know the colour of the work assigned to it. The common presumption is that the colour is Orange. Is it not true that the members of the team are conferring and jointly share responsibility for any decision reached? Unhappily, that may be an illusion. The reality is that team members may have reached agreement, which is not the same as a decision. Relevant here is the story about the husband and wife who have parcelled out their respective roles; the husband decides on whether the nation should have atomic weapons and the wife decides on which school the children should attend. Here the word decision is being used in two different senses. The wife would be accountable for the decision reached on the choice of school. If she made an unfortunate choice, her husband could blame her. But has her husband really made a decision about atomic weapons? Can he be held accountable for what happens when atomic weapons are used or banned? It would be more correct to say that her husband had expressed a view. It did not really constitute a decision because there was no output. There is therefore a distinction to be drawn between an agreement based on concurring views on the one hand and shared decisions on the other, just as there is between a personal view on the one hand

and on the other a personal decision that leads to personal action. Yellow and Orange work both involve criteria for assessing outcomes. Colours remove the ambiguities that otherwise creep into the use of verbal language.

Consider now the question of decision-making. It would seem that there are only three conditions under which effective decisions can be made. There is, of course, Yellow work where accountability for whatever decision is made rests with a single person. Yellow and Green makes the decision-making process slightly more social. One person consults another before making the decision. Responsibility for that decision remains an individual matter but modifying the purity of Yellow work helps to make it more effective. The social quality of decision-making reaches its zenith in Orange work, which needs to be based on the carefully chosen team. Thereafter, increasing the sociability of the process does not improve the quality of decision-making but in fact detracts from it. As numbers involved in the decision-making process increase, a condition is created that has the merits of neither Yellow nor Orange work. There are several conditions under which poor decisions are likely to be made and few that favour good decisions (see Figure 9).

Not all teams are in the decision-making business. Teams that are set up to reach or exchange views are essentially engaged in Green work. Such work can seldom justify itself in the effective use of person-time except for short engagements. Unfortunately, due to ambiguities in the use of language Green work is often presumed by a designated team to constitute Orange work. Once team members discover that what they agreed after conferring is not treated as a shared decision, disillusion sets in.

Where cross-functional teams are set up, it is important to establish from the outset whether they are in the business of Green work or Orange work. If cross-functional teams are in the latter category they should be formed according to the principles of good team-building. That means they should not be put forward as representatives just because they have a particular background but should be selected on the basis of the type of contribution they are likely to make. Admittedly, there are many occasions that justify people from different departments and backgrounds congregating in order to exchange information and views. These hardly constitute teams and such planned encounters are better treated as meetings along the lines suggested in Chapter 6. Such meetings should be of limited duration and can be exempted from the stricter code and regulation that true teamwork demands.

Work roles communicate the nature of the work being demanded. For the core managerial skills to be mastered, this means gaining an understanding of the difference between a task and a responsibility and the difference between personal and prescribed work on the one hand and, on the other, work that is shared or interactive. It may be less obvious but it is equally important that the competent employee should know the difference too. It is not easy to do a job well if one is uncertain about what a manager really requires. And if the manager is unable to express adequately what is needed, the job becomes doubly difficult to perform to a satisfactory standard. It is here that we have found how quickly employees take to the colour-language for expressing work roles. They readily discuss among themselves whether work is Blue or Yellow, Green or Orange. They are most fond of citing Pink work, for evidently there is a lot of it about.

People are at their most effective in their work roles when they feel free from Pink work and when the work roles they are given correspond with their preferred work roles and the roles their colleagues assess to be strong. In other words, they do not feel their time is being used unproductively, they like the work they do and others think they do it well. There is here an echo of our experiences with team roles. In *Team Roles at Work* I noted that those rated as effective people tended to have coherent profiles; that is, their profiles as ranked on nine team roles corresponded well with the way in which those roles were ranked by their work associates. Conversely, those given poor ratings presented a picture of incompatible profiles, where there was a conflict between the perception of the self and the self as perceived by others. When people are in the right role, their fulfilment is widely perceived and they are averse to taking on work for which they are unsuited or which they feel has no outcome. So also the same position applies with work roles. Individuals need to be aware of how much they feel drawn to each of the seven colour areas and how that sense of affinity corresponds with how others see them performing in those areas. That is the road for establishing maturity at work.

There is a good case then for learning to use work-role language proactively. It is a common experience that new employees starting in their first job are confused about what is expected of them. They find it difficult to interpret the information being given because there is no standard language to convey what is meant. So when an individual is assigned work, uncertainties can be met with questions. 'How do you want me to handle this? Do you want me to look after this area generally or just on this occasion? Is there anyone else who should come into this?' By a series of interlocking questions the sophisticated new entrant may be able to cope adequately with the demands of a naïve manager and to show initiative in the process. By inference, it may then be established whether the work is Blue, Yellow, Green or Orange. Of course, such a device is less satisfactory than for both parties to be aware of and to use the same colour language in communicating the demands and nature of the work in hand and in prospect.

The original model for the conveyance and modification of work roles was through assignment by the manager to the jobholder. This was difficult to bring about without the aid of a facilitator, who was found to play a valuable part in relaying information back to the manager in a reverse of the conventional information-giving process. In that way the manager would be made aware of the realities of the current job situation and so be freed from hanging on to a fixed image of the job as it had been known in the past. Managers were then better placed to hasten the processes of change and to make better use of existing resources.

That process certainly made an advance but was still limited by an over-reliance on intervention by the manager. Response to an improved system could still be slow, especially if the manager was busy. Yet once team members understood the language of work roles and saw the benefits which an improved system could yield, to that extent they could act on the information themselves and initiate improvements in the way in which resources were deployed. In other words, after a period of learning, mature team members could adjust to the vicissitudes of demands placed upon them more speedily and efficiently.

The mature team can be gauged by its learning on three fundamental counts. The first is the team's knowledge of itself. Team members need close mutual understanding in terms of team roles and what they can expect from each other. Secondly, the mature team needs also to understand the basic divisions in the demands of work and be able to communicate to each other in terms of work roles. Thirdly, the mature team needs to cultivate a capacity for internal negotiation, where work roles are treated as the primary consideration and team roles as the secondary consideration. The work must be done even if team-role sacrifices have to be made. However, if work roles can be distributed in a way that corresponds with the characteristic team roles, skills and interests of its various members, a happy situation exists.

Yet the hard reality is that some discrepancy is likely to exist. Life seldom fits the blueprint of an ideal world. Any one individual may need to make sacrifices for the greater good. Just as the show must go on in show business, so the work must go on in work business. The mature team will be ready to face up to crises and contingencies. It will not wait for the manager to say yea or nay but will take action how and where it is required.

The mature team can act as a beacon, presenting a model of ideal practice for those striving against the odds for better decision-making based on closer collaboration between suitable people. Such possibilities do not depend on the members themselves alone. The mature team is best fostered, nurtured and brought into being within a mature organization. If such teams are infrequently found or are dissolved before that maturity can begin to show, the explanation may be that the historical and critical political moment for their emergence has not yet arrived.

12

The paradox of management

Management in the present era can be represented as a Janus figure – with two heads looking in opposite directions. In its more forward-looking view management believes in competition within a free market. Competition is healthy; it leads to progress; it operates in the public interest. But management's other head faces away from competition; it looks for standardization; it jealously guards its own centralized decision-making; it stifles competition within the organization; it structures work to ensure that every aspect of its corporate activity is subject to a sole authority, with each level being accountable to the next one higher up. How is it that these two heads belong to the same body?

Logically it is difficult to be an advocate of both centralization and decentralization, of authoritative leadership and close team-work, of individual performance-related pay and sharing in the benefits of success. Equally, one cannot both support rigid job descriptions and flexible jobs, nor a commitment to a holistic management of resources along with the systematic fragmentation and ultimate erosion of responsibilities.

There is one explanation that probably covers all these paradoxes. My belief is that organizational effectiveness is pulling in one direction and genetic pressures in another. The human disposition to organize has much in common with all mammals that operate in groups. The behaviour of the group much depends on the alpha male. The alpha male will be the largest in the herd. Large antlers help in battles for dominance with other males. The winner takes the available females. In the case of humans, the winner takes the money. Top salaries become the expected prize of conquest.

Humans do not possess antlers but physical size facilitates human dominance. Some American research has revealed the greater average height and weight of presidents relative to middle managers within business organizations. Physical size has had an undoubted impact on the history of the United States. Originally, scattered English colonies along the East Coast of the United States had no sense of American consciousness. They saw England as the mother country. After the Boston Tea Party and the clash between the colonists and the British Redcoats in Massachusetts, the northern colonists looked south for allies. The Virginians looked with suspicion on the Bostonians and on the idea of an American Confederation until the insightful John Adams nominated the tallest Virginian, George Washington, to be their President. Washington then made his mark as the dominant leader, physically well suited to the wielding of personal power. I often ask Americans who visit Cambridge to tell me about the origins of the Stars and Stripes. Whatever their explanation, I surprise them when I conduct them into Little St Mary's Church, where, on turning left as they enter, they see a crest belonging to the Washington family, containing stars and stripes and an eagle at its top.

Not only do leaders of large organizations act like solo leaders but others expect them to behave in that way. Chapter 3 brought out the difference between the psychology of the team and the psychology of the group. The issues of dominance are even more prominent when larger numbers gather than when small groups form. People look for a King, a President or a Messiah. The prevalence of this phenomenon raises the question why. Is it cultural? Is it a force representing social adaptation so that the person most fitted to lead naturally emerges? It is difficult to find anything more convincing in accounting for a wide range of phenomena than the simple explanation of genetic programming. There is here a certain consistency. Even at the very earliest ages at which individual behaviour can exert itself, siblings manifest rivalry. Squabbling and fighting will be found among males, even in the most well conducted families where pacifism may be highly valued. In adolescence, tempered aggression is often turned towards parents. Among young men that aggression continues on its outward path. Taking a social form, it shows itself against other groups. A warrior class is then ready to do battle if only an enemy can be found. Among older males battle-readiness is more subdued but a strong internal force still presses against rivals.

In terms of the struggle for dominance alpha females do not figure as strongly as alpha males. Among almost all mammals the males are larger than females and therefore have a physical advantage. Where females hunt as a pack, as with lionesses, so that size is a relative matter, the alpha female becomes the effective organizer. Alpha female dominance is never something to be ignored, since it will manifest itself when no dominant male is present or can be easily overcome, as witnessed in a television documentary featuring film of a solo female elephant in a private game park. Set among a herd of buffaloes, the female elephant took over the lead position after killing the dominant male buffalo and maintained the same pose. A female historical figure, usually of royal lineage, has occasionally behaved like our solo female elephant, but in general the contest is between males.

In human organizations the absence of a dominant leader creates a niche waiting to be filled. The struggle for power has been the centrepiece of much human history. Potential rivals in the succession stakes have been poisoned, assassinated or removed by means of quasi-judicial execution. That is the background to be borne in mind as we turn our attention from history and politics to business and the public service. Yet here there is a difference. History and politics are about power and the factors that create it, while business and the public service have to take in effectiveness. Those who run a business are accountable to the stakeholders (being the shareholders, the employees and, in another sense, customers and suppliers) for the results achieved. Those who control public services are accountable in a democratic society to an electorate.

Now the question that has to be asked is how the genetic impulse to achieve dominance impacts on the overriding need to create effectiveness. It is here that the language of work roles can help us to resolve the problem. A central feature of all organizations lies in their decision-making processes. There are two typical failings of the solo leader as created in the genetic struggle for dominance. The first is that big decisions on complex matters do not receive the detailed attention and range of alternative options that they warrant. Where effectiveness is concerned, the desired colour of work bears a strong relationship to the level of risk and complexity (see Figure 10). It is this model that has formed the cornerstone of the advice my colleagues and I have given on how any cluster of jobs should be organized.

Yet for all that, dominant leaders are prone to make impulsive decisions and to disregard advisers. In other words, decisions are based on Yellow work in situations where they would be better served by Orange work. Orange work is roundtable work, where the most senior person ideally now becomes just one member of a team. That adjustment demands modesty and humility, qualities difficult to nurture and display by those usually intent on personal advancement.

The second most common failing of dominant leaders is the proneness to overrule others in their own area of responsibility. Here Yellow work has been passed to another executive but its meaning has now been negated. In effect, the dominant leader takes back the Yellow work and the now deprived executive is left with work of no particular colour. That must be the explanation of why those who work close to a dominant leader so often appear more indecisive than those who occupy less senior positions but have clearer orbits of responsibility.

There is a third factor of concern about a genetically based hierarchy. A hierarchy that depends heavily on one alpha male introduces a high degree of unpredictability. That is because individuals vary so much in their abilities. There will be cases where there is no problem. Some who have reached the summit of the hierarchy and have exercised the power to overcome opposition on the way possess singular talents. By seeing the whole picture they steer the ship in the right direction. Sheer talent can compensate for a poor management style. The deficiencies of that style are soon exposed in anyone of inferior ability. The worst scenario is where a person of limited ability occupies a position of power and oversees others whose abilities exceed those of the leader. That inversion of an effective hierarchy is the setting that throughout history has set the scene for the tyrant and for tragedy. So is it the person or the organizational model which is the more important?

We must now return to the theme of this book and ask what effect human genetic tendencies can have on work roles. My belief is that archetypal forces push larger organizations into inefficient modes of operation. A poor organizational model in the end distorts work roles. Responsibilities are diminished. There is an over-dependence on a single person whose weaknesses cannot be corrected or managed by others.

If, as I suspect, the genetic force is ever-present, the permanence of any gains in improved organization cannot be assumed. Reversion to a natural human organization, i.e. a led hierarchy, is always a possibility. A well-established hierarchy will cling to its favoured procedures, whatever progress is made in the effectiveness of alternative operations at the local level. One head of Janus will be looking in one direction but the other head will have a fixated gaze in the other.

Here two instances from the history of dynamic systems we had pioneered in team roles and work roles (with use of the appropriate software) offer some useful lessons. Two large public bodies provided flagships that served to illustrate the best of operational practice. In the one case, after a number of years of successful progress, the situation changed overnight. A new Chief Executive along with a new HR Director brought an instant return to the older orthodoxy with which they were more familiar. In a second case, the practices pioneered in one department eventually proved incompatible with practices being followed in the rest of the organization. In the ensuing tug-of-war the major ongoing practices, sensing the threat, re-established their hold on the organization as a whole.

Where pioneering progress runs into a setback, experience has shown that all is not lost. Commonly there are two outcomes. One is the diaspora. Pioneers leave and transfer their skills and experience to another scene of employment. Staggered progress can have the effect of aiding dissemination and widening the scope of innovation. The other outcome is that what has started and has become suppressed merely continues unofficially. A company may have a structure but it is also a social organism and it is the social system that preserves what it values. The flag on a flagship comes down but the ship continues to sail. It will take time before there is a big enough momentum to change the paradigm on which organizations are founded.

Top-down bureaucracies are not going to be easy to reform. Human biology imposes its own order. But the criteria have now changed. Effectiveness is what is demanded. New models of human organization are needed to replace hierarchical bureaucracies. In the next chapter I will consider what new guidelines and pointers might serve us for the future.

13

The superorganism – a model for work organization

The potential that people can bring to a work situation often corresponds poorly with what they are able to deliver. The performance of people at work is constrained by how a job is set up. The job can be the starting-point from which all other things follow. In reality, its emergence and shape depend on other forces, reflecting the demands of the market or the need to provide a service in line with the nature and philosophy of the employing body. If jobs are not formulated to hang together as a dynamic entity within a coherent system, the effectiveness of the whole will be severely weakened.

When people associate in work as individuals or in small groups, the roles they take up come about through discussion and trade-offs. So a reasonable amount of adjustment applies within the system whereby jobs are tackled. It is another matter when jobs are forged within larger population densities and formations. Then the roles are cast within a framework that still reflects the way in which gregarious mammals behave in general. In other words, all roles are influenced by degrees of dominance and submission. Behavioural pecking orders or contests between contenders for dominance of the pack are much in evidence and generate winners and losers. Large-scale organization and personal dominance in a literate society then give birth to multi-layered bureaucracy. Admittedly, such a pattern has its undoubted strengths; for example, hierarchical organization is capable of marshalling and channelling effort and resources on a large-scale in a given direction.

However, traditional static structures are looking increasingly out of place in the modern world. If broader aims are to be achieved and work roles in systems made more productive and personally rewarding, the best hope must be to create some form of paradigm shift. That is clearly going to be difficult where the goal of any basic reform entails modifying what is taken as normal human behaviour. If power corrupts and organizations create power opportunities, the prospects for change would not seem very bright.

Yet, for all that, there is a glimmer of hope. Those who head large, highly structured, organizations are now increasingly being held accountable for their effectiveness. In both the public and private sectors the priority is to deliver greater value from existing resources. Here it is just possible that a well-educated society may respond to the challenge. To do so would mean recognizing and facing up to the unfavourable elements rooted in genetically driven modes of social behaviour and to strive to move in a different direction. That movement is being speeded up as more and more women take up senior appointments and so change the arena in which contests of alpha male strength are being played out. The prospect of making a paradigm shift is greater than might have been imagined.

With the aim of glimpsing into the future I have thought fit to look to the social insects, which include ants, bees, wasps and termites. In a previous book, *The Coming Shape of Organization*, I examined some of the salient behaviours of the social insects and the mechanisms by which they were achieved. It has been a view of scientists specializing in this area that one key to the evolutionary success of the social insects lies in their capacity to act like a multi-cellular organism, or more concisely, as a superorganism. What this means is that the character of the whole body retains its basic stability through a decentralized system involving the autonomous yet co-operative interaction of its parts. This collectivist mechanism for survival has been evolving on this planet over a huge span of time, estimated by some researchers, in the case of ants, as being in excess of 50 million years. That makes the history of human evolution appear almost insignificant in comparison.

Now bear in mind that sociobiologists maintain that evolution can focus on individuals, kin and the group. Ants, it seems, have followed the last path and have adopted to this end *reciprocal altruism.* If every member of a colony is designed to act in a way that benefits all other members, huge advantages accrue to the colony as a whole. And because worker ants do everything for the common good – protecting their food source and the reproductive queen are their foremost tasks – they sacrifice themselves at an instant's notice. There are ants that have squirt guns in their heads or explode like a bomb when invaders find the tunnel entrance to the queen's quarters. But usually the contribution that each worker ant makes is less dramatic, being based on a finely attuned balance in roles that the colony needs for its survival and prosperity.

Ants have also learned the benefits of symbiosis, deriving mutual benefit from their association with other insects and with plants. Plants lure ants with nectar and other foods while acting themselves as pollinators. Birds engage in a similar function. But the symbiotic relationship in the case of ants extends to protection. Ants feed on sweet sap or nectar from certain plants and in return defend the same plants from pests. In one remarkable variant of this relationship, the Camponotus ant prefers the nectar when it has been digested and secreted by another insect, which itself escapes the ant's wrath.

The evolution of organizational sophistication in the social insects has even been aided by co-operation as between different species. For example, American scientists using DNA techniques have provided evidence that ants farming mushrooms have continued to develop their skills. Research, published in *Science,* shows that some ants are able to cultivate eight different types of mushroom, though they grow only one at a time. Different ant species exchange information and learn to cultivate mushrooms favoured by other species. There are known to be at least 12 000 species of ants. Ants farm, herd (3000 species of insects have been domesticated) and they evidently negotiate. To sum up, ants may be reckoned to be the world's leading proponents of mutualism. They have perfected all the refinements and benefits we associate with *win–win* relationships.

The superfamily of Hymenoptera, which includes bees, wasps and ants, contains some 20 000 species. So there is huge scope for competition in effectiveness. The termites belong to another large yet unrelated family called the Isoptera. The termites are remarkable for the size and complexity of their constructions. For example, in Macrotermes some nests are virtually cathedrals in clay, reaching six or seven metres high, that is, 600 times the size of a worker. A variety of specialist trades make such a construction possible. Among the Apicotermes termites huge underground nests are constructed with stacked horizontal chambers connected by helix-shaped vertical passages that are used as spiral staircases. The ability to deploy thermal control and ventilating arrangements of a high order is shared by both ants and termites. There are many distinctions within the families of Hymenoptera and Isoptera that give rise to many different species, each well adapted to the exploitation of a particular set of environmental conditions. Yet for all their differences, similar organizational features of all these families illustrate the common principles revealed by evolutionary parallelism.

The refined capacities of the social insects in general are made possible through the range and volume of information they receive through their sense-receptors. They respond to absolute and gradient differences in odour, taste, sight, light, temperature and pheromones (the chemical agents affecting behaviour), processing and integrating all this information in brains that are notably large in relation to their bodies. The capacity of the social insects to undertake a wide variety of tasks is further aided by the existence of specialized castes. This division of labour varies greatly between species but is notable in that it is achieved without incurring the economic costs of rigidity. Workers can change the tasks they take on during stages in their life-span. Yet there is still further flexibility within that development for speeding up or slowing down the rate at which they change work roles according to external circumstances. In short, the complexity of the social organization of the social insects is as intricate as the immense cathedral-like habitations some of them are capable of constructing.

If what I have touched on only briefly creates a sense of wonder, we should now turn to human organization, at which point one may ask whether these two different worlds have any points of common interest. The problem is that while humans and the social insects may be expert communicators, we cannot communicate with each other for we are built to use quite different language systems. When humans cannot share a common language, we are prone to *anthropomorphize* (projecting our own qualities into other creatures). English literature is full of classic stories from the *Wind in the Willows* and Rudyard Kipling's *Jungle Book* to Beatrix Potter's *Jemima Puddleduck* and her many other books that weave stories round her notable animal personalities. Such books have world-wide appeal. (I have been struck by the number of Japanese visitors to the museum dedicated to her works in the Lake District). Mickey and Minney Mouse and many other quasi-human Walt Disney characters are recipients of even more conspicuous fame and live on in theme parks frequented by huge numbers of visitors from all continents.

The tendency to anthropomorphize invades even more technical and scientific assessments of other creatures. The key figure in a colony of the social insects is called the *queen*. One's thoughts naturally turn to an *Alice in Wonderland* figure who might exclaim 'Off with their heads'. In fact, it is difficult to think of any similarity, except specimen singularity in a populous brood, that allows any valid comparison between an insect queen and a royal personage. The insect queen wields no personal power and has a more limited range of responses than other members of the colony. The queen has no function other than that of a specialist breeder and a secretor of a liquid that those who attend her find attractive. Any suggestion of her title carrying a special place at the top of a hierarchy is entirely false. The social insects are not in the hierarchy business. Instead, they operate at a wide range of different levels in an intricate network. In contrast, human stories about animals are all about the relative power of the respective players and this is what creates the excitement. While humans have this proclivity for being self-centred in their perceptions of the natural world, perhaps the natural world has something to teach humans. Instead of indulging in anthropomorphism, let us move in the opposite direction and *entomorphize*. In other words, rather than look at the world of the social insects through human eyes, let us do so through the eyes of the social insects. Let us imagine that human society had gone through another million years of evolution. Only the social forms most fitted to survive would be left. What would we be like? We do not have the experience to judge. Ant and Bee would be better placed to express a view, because their societies have been through just such a collective experience.

If we were to take two major public concerns – health and education – and we were to explain current predicaments in human society, what advice would we expect Ant and Bee to convey? Almost certainly they would be critical of our multi-tiered hierarchies. 'Why', they would say 'does a Minister impose policies on professionals when professionals know more about the subject than the Minister?' An obvious response would be to declare that the Minister is responsible for doling out public money and is therefore acting in the public interest. I am sure that Bee would not be convinced and would point out that while humans have money bees have honey. The queen bee does not control the distribution of the honey. The honey like the money is collected for common use. Honey is drawn from the common store but its distribution in practice is spread locally in an equitable and fairly even way.

Now let us suppose we were to act in a way that Ant and Bee might consider functionally effective. The implication for us is that the role of Government would be to act as a specialist collector of money (a fairly technical matter in human society) and then to preside over its equitable distribution. As Ant and Bee live in a world of sophisticated communication; they would expect humans to be aware of what happened to the money and for that information to be widely spread and publicly available. That would not be an unreasonable assumption. Now that information technology has changed our lives, we should be almost as well informed as Ant and Bee. Such are the recommendations that would spring from *entomorphism*.

Now let us follow this sequence of thought and consider how feasible it would be to act on that advice. It would mean that hospitals and schools would get a chunk of money and the community would expect them to use it to best effect. But how would it actually be used? Almost certainly it would be used in different ways. Would that be an advantage or a disadvantage? It would be an advantage in many respects. There would be an informed comparison on the consequences of using given sums of money in different ways. The free circulation of that information would be a spur to progress. Each community would be better informed in acting as a pressure group to ensure that the use of the honey, I beg your pardon money, best matched local needs.

But what about the disadvantages? The pretence that every community was receiving, and should receive, exactly the same service would be undermined. Politicians would have to sacrifice the claim that a fully comprehensive Health Service would ensure equality in health treatment. Personally, I cannot see that as a disadvantage, for I take the view that the public stance of politicians on this issue is illusory. With an ageing population, the huge growth in the range of sophisticated and expensive treatment technically available and the shortage of medical expertise in many specialist fields, there is no equality. Nor do most senior professionals in the field that I have encountered believe there is. Nor is there any prospect, in my view, that inequalities will be removed in the foreseeable future.

The best prospect is that well-selected teams of professionals and suitable non-professionals will ensure that their local communities get the best value for money. In the field of education similar principles apply. The education that any community feels best suits its needs depends on that population itself, its aptitudes, its cultural interests, its employment prospects and the skills of its teaching staff. The most suitable format is best unravelled at the local level. These people will no doubt, when suitably informed, wish to take account of what goes on elsewhere.

I fail to see what could possibly be wrong with Ant and Bee's advice. What I do fear, however, is that we are locked into a system of hierarchical bureaucracy that everyone is aware is failing but from which we cannot easily extricate ourselves. At this point we may need to take a step back. Instead of focusing on solutions on a grand scale that are out of reach, it might be better to establish some starting principles of how to cope with groups of increasing size and with the arrangement of jobs within them. In a world whose population is growing steadily it is a problem from which we will not be able to escape for long.

Chapter

14

From groups to
supergroups

As I have attempted to show, humans are not genetically
equipped to function effectively in large groups. That is hardly
surprising, for the tendency for large groups to malfunction
needs to be considered against the origin of the human species.
Evolution has designed us for existence in a different ecosystem
from the one we now occupy. If only a small slice of time could be
removed from the total span of human genetic history, and we
were to press *fastback*, we could find ourselves close to our
primeval roots. By nature we would be much as we are now but
living in a less densely populated landscape. Small co-operative
groups would be busily engaged in hunting, gathering and some
limited planting. Such a world would invite adventure and
exploration, where survival demands a spread of work roles to
match a limited but varying spread of challenges. In such an
environment small-scale society provides exactly the right setting
in which teams can be created, comprising people who know
each other intimately and choose to work in close association.

However, small-scale society offers limited scope in what can be
achieved. Larger groups, once formed, may encounter difficulties

that go with size but they also open up new areas for human advancement. Size offers economies of scale and opens up the possibilities of using a wider spread of specialized work roles. Such a formula provides the basis for building epic wonders, like the Great Wall of China and the pyramids of Egypt, for undertaking huge projects in the irrigation and cultivation of arid lands and, less constructively, for engaging in vast military campaigns. If people follow some common purpose and acquiesce in being treated en masse, humans are capable of monumental accomplishments.

However, none of this is possible without a particular form of social order. When people come together in numbers too large or unselected in composition to form a team, the need to secure cohesion becomes paramount along with the need to regain that sense of lost personal intimacy that small-scale society provides. Here the way is opened for leadership based on the combination of power and a personality cult. Whoever becomes the leader can make unquestioned decisions without being subject to limiting restrictions. Solo leaders can authorize and deploy large numbers of people in an orderly manner for a given purpose to great effect. The work roles intrinsic to a hierarchical society have a distinctive pattern, aggregating Yellow work in a single powerful person, with little or very limited personal accountability, combined with a proliferation of Green work for courtiers and sycophants and Blue work for their underlings.

The solo leader may be there by birthright, may have risen through a power struggle or that ascendancy may rest on merit, owing much to some conspicuous set of skills, especially in communication, persuasion and political understanding. But the benefits offered by a talented solo leader in a large group are prone to be nullified, as team-role theory affirms, by an associated character weakness. Outstanding qualities are not uniformly spread, even in a talented person. A single strength at the level of distinction often operates at the expense of another. So the work roles which that solo leader takes up are likely to be dominated by personal preferences rather than an awareness of overt needs. It follows that progress and setbacks will be coupled together. While instances abound of sudden reversals in fortunes among solo industrial leaders, they have become almost the norm in politics and in history.

Consider now the broad question of human folly and the conditions under which it arises. There is a saying *'If a folly is large enough, it will be invisible'*. It is a remarkable assertion, but I am bound to say that it rings true. Where I have encountered it, I have been reminded of *groupthink*, discussed in Chapter 3. The domination of a large group by someone with authority promotes consensus. While small mistakes are easily spotted and corrected, since they are more likely to excite individual attention, large mistakes are shrouded by the uncertainties about the surrounding circumstances. Not enough people possess detailed information or have been personally involved in the events. The assumption is that if the leader favours it and others have endorsed it (often an illusion in itself), the decision must be right. Large mistakes commonly arise, yet are least likely to be detected and corrected, in closely controlled hierarchies. Any perceived and reported blunder would reflect on the leader, cause the leader to lose face and pose a clear threat to the Established Order. So the blunder develops an immunity against public recognition.

Here I can recall a number of CEOs of undulating fortunes, whose period in power has ultimately been associated with a notable downturn in business. The skill of remaining in office often calls on the capacity for giving a plausible explanation for mistakes. If the hoped for results have not yet arrived, it will be argued that the basic policy is right and only awaits more vigorous pursuit. Examples abound in the military field from campaigns that have eventually turned into disasters. If bombardment has not brought about the defeat of the enemy, the reason is that not enough bombs, missiles or troops have been despatched. Large mistakes are seldom due to the reasons ostensibly given by those in responsibility, but have a more basic explanation: they are generally the price paid for operating with an insufficient spread of human skills in complex areas.

The penalty for too narrow a focus is that important problems are left unrecognized. As groups get larger and issues become more complex, the problems mount and defy the overall attention of a single person. The much enlarged group begins to lose its viability and capacity for long-term survival. The only way out of growing difficulty is for the social organization to alight upon a systems change involving the devolution of responsibilities, so relieving pressure on the nominal leader.

There are various ways in which this has come about in history. One is through attenuation in the powers of a previously mighty person on the grounds that an Emperor or God–King is too holy to engage in secular matters. Japanese Emperors and Tibetan Dalai Lamas provide historical instances of *supreme* leaders who have lived at times in virtual poverty, as their secular powers have been diminished through an over-dependence on underlings. A second route follows the knock-on effects of hedonism. A Sultan's time may be largely consumed in a harem and in the planning and building of a luxurious palace, so allowing political leadership to pass to Viziers, eunuchs and others. One of the features of the long-lasting Ottoman Empire was the part played by slave boys, carefully educated, selected and groomed to engage in the administrative functions of empire. Being unlikely to pose any serious threat to the dynasty, they rose to take on major responsibilities. A third route for diminishing the powers of the solo leader is through constitutional reform. The Roman Republic provides just such an instance, as it emerged from the ashes of the Etruscan civilization and used *duality* as a form of constitutional innovation. As a safeguard against the preceding tyranny of kings, or the danger that any one member of rival patrician families might gain absolute power, offices were paired. Under this principle of *collegiality*, there were two *consuls* (chief magistrates), two *questors* (chief financial officers) and so on. That system lasted throughout the period associated with the *glory of Rome*, only becoming eroded with the growth and spread of the Roman Empire. (A close parallel of this duality in modern industrial corporations is the division of powers between a chairman and a chief executive or between two joint managing directors). England provides a further example of a constitutional device for limiting the power of a single person following the Civil War between the Cavaliers (monarchists) and the Roundheads (parliamentarians). The transfer of powers from the monarchy to the Lords (significantly called 'Peers') and Commons jointly assembled in Parliament produced a paradigm shift in the functions of the state, and continued even when a King was finally restored to the throne. Then the monarch became largely a figurehead.

In all these cases, a device has been found for redistributing responsibilities normally invested in a single person. The redistribution of Yellow work, mixed in the case of Peers with some growth in Orange work, allows empires to outlast any one individual's lifetime and so to form a wider baseline on which social and historical stability can be constructed.

Size operates on a continuum and in its higher levels generates pressures that affect the stability of the whole. As the group becomes progressively enlarged it reaches a stage where it can no longer operate effectively as a large body of like-minded people subject to the dominance of a single personality. Size eventually creates a new *gestalt*, turning the image of a group into an abstraction, allowing its members to share through rituals an image of collectivity, often aided by some form of mythology. That will allow a *nation* to include peoples of different ethnic, linguistic and religious traditions, who share little in common. What gives a nation an unquestionable reality rests on the way it fulfils its overall needs through its *working* institutions, including Education, Justice, Health, the Armed Services and so on. These constituent bodies have designated work roles, which are discharged in a corporate form.

The body that can generate corporate work roles is too large and multifaceted to be led effectively by a single person. The *mega-group* undergoes substantial strains where it operates merely in the same style as a large group. Many mega-groups function in that way. They become top-heavy, bureaucratic and they stifle local initiatives. That is because work roles are distributed in personal terms through an inner court of privileged people who are close to the person in power. Some of these people are recipients of Green work rather than Yellow work. Only by keeping close to the Master can his wishes be enacted.

If the mega-group is to retain its viability, responsibilities will need to be spread. Then much Yellow work passes not to a person but to an institution. Such a transformation of a mega-group into a *supergroup* generates a new form of dynamism by redistributing functions. Here comparison can be made with a living organism. Organs, with their capacity for autonomic functioning, prolong the life of the human body. So also, in their political context, they perpetuate political entities by offering constitutional protection against the disturbance that can follow the death of a leader, which could threaten death to the organism as a whole. History has shown how the intervention of an established priesthood can ensure, at a time of crisis, moral authority and a smooth succession. Set against that advantage in political organizations is the price paid for this diffusion of power. Power and authority can grow unrelentingly in the separate organs of the supergroup until its corporate dynamism is lost and it begins to revert to the rigidities that characterize the mega-group. For example, the belief systems of society, enshrined for safe keeping in the priesthood, may be retained there permanently and are not negotiable. Accountability is internally rather than externally focused. This new source of power, being no longer subject to external constraints, can bring with it tragic consequences. Among the Aztecs of Central America, the rate of human sacrifices was speeded up during crises in order to appease angry gods, so precluding other approaches to the afflictions of a suffering society. In contemporary times contraception, as an answer to over-population, is widely opposed in many parts of the world for reasons of institutionalized belief. There is a conservatism that typically becomes embedded in each of the separate organs of the mega-group that debars its potential transformation into a supergroup.

Even Education proves subject to this law. Its valued contribution in the outsider's view is that it can create good citizens, facilitate entry into jobs and provide the scientific, entrepreneurial and business skills that guarantee continuing prosperity in society itself. But Education will not necessarily see it in that way. Its own internal imperatives will take precedence over the wider objectives. Learning, knowledge and academic qualifications remain the leading and sometimes the sole priorities. It is of less concern to Education that it may cast on to the labour market an oversupply of educated people, poorly equipped in attitude and skills to contribute to societal needs, and an undersupply of those who have skills to meet general demand. The Law, as another organ of society, is equally disposed to pursue its own preferred path. On the one hand, it provides a laudable basis for settling disputes and giving confidence in Justice. On the other hand, the Law is claimed on popular reckoning to be an ass: in other words, it works according to its own rules and precedents irrespective of what the public may deem sensible. Similarly, the Police Authority may focus on catching criminals and the prisons on securely incarcerating them, while the wider goal of producing more law-abiding citizens is left aside.

Mega-groups can certainly improve their effectiveness by setting up corporate functions that can serve the totality of the organism in the direction of a supergroup. But such an organizational improvement, valued though it may be, cannot be equated with the efficacy of superorganisms in the social insect world. A true superorganism will be held together by its *interacting* dynamic functions by the creation of system stability that does not rely on external interventions.

The true superorganism may be difficult to achieve in a world full of competitive human beings. Still the intermediate possibility is there. A supergroup can use teamwork at a basic operating level, can value dynamic interaction and maximize the flow of information between its members. Hierarchy can be used for orderly and strategic purposes rather than for purposes of extending power over others. In the same way that a team can develop into a mature team, so also a supergroup can refine its internal functioning style to bring it closer to that of a superorganism.

15

Some steps in the right direction

Very few large organizations I have encountered behave like supergroups, but I will mention one in the private sector that falls into this area: the Toyota Motor Manufacturing Company (UK) Ltd at Derby. Toyota declares in its philosophy that it *strives to achieve an organization in which all employees can develop to their full potential. Teamwork is an essential element of Toyota's operating philosophy, believing that a well co-ordinated group can accomplish far more than the sum of individual efforts.*

Words are often blithely chosen, while corresponding with little that happens in reality. But in the case of Toyota, the philosophy and the practice work closely together. For example, this is one of the few companies I know that distinguishes between a team and a group. The basis of that distinction is size. A team will comprise not more than five people. A team leader will work with the team and will assist team members when they encounter a problem and be seen as a *brother*. Four team leaders will report to a group leader, responsible for, on average, 25 people, for disciplinary issues and for planning, and projected as *father to the group*. A senior group leader will be responsible for a shift, while the term *manager* is retained for a broader set of roles. For purposes of remuneration, a variety of engineers, specialists and administrators fall within each of these grades in a broad-banded system, which will allow an engineer, for example, to be free to move between different branches of engineering without running into any organizational or financial impediments. The absence of any system of job description or job evaluation facilitates flexibility in the deployment of people. While the lack of any means of projecting the content of a job is admitted to be one of the downsides of the system, this price is considered to be small and one worth paying for the flexibility which this freedom of constraints allows. The emphasis on flexibility is supported by the use made of team roles, and of its associated technology *Interplace*, at management and intermediate levels in dealing with the composition and development of teams.

Team members play an active part in contributing to added value. Here there are three Japanese concepts that underlie the prevailing philosophy. The first is *kaizen*, which literally means change for good, or in freer translation indicates the emphasis on continuous improvement. The second is *muda*, which stands for waste, classified according to seven different viewpoints from which it can be tackled. *Muda* deals largely with the physical side of waste, as might be expected in an engineering mass production company, and in that respect is related to person-time. Here the involvement of people in the process plays an important part in removing waste. *Jidoka* is another notable concept and relates to 'automation with a human touch', so extending human powers into the operation of automated lines. One example of its application is *andon*, which allows a team member on the line to signal a fault. That will prompt a team leader to render assistance. Should that assistance fail to remedy the problem by a certain point in the line, the line will stop. Hence a great measure of trust is put on each team member.

One comment made to me was that Toyota companies have the same feel about them everywhere: the culture is all-pervasive. I have contrasted this in my mind with other establishments where the culture depends very much on who is boss at the time. Herein lies the contrast between solo-led hierarchies, together with their bureaucratic procedures, and companies that are activated by the organic nature of their systems.

That change can take place when structures are fully replaced with processes, when people move between teams and contribute from a widening perspective. It will take place when a social mechanism exists for this to happen. It may seem strange to say so, but I believe social insects enjoy more career development and more freedom than most people who are cast into *jobs* in hierarchical companies. That is because work roles are *imposed* on people, while the social insects are in continuous working interaction with their environment.

If one considers the public sector, it is difficult to cite an example of a corporate body that acts like a supergroup. This is not to say there are not some excellently managed hospitals, schools, councils and public utilities. The problem arises because these bodies do not have adequate control over their responsibilities and they suffer a confused system of accountability. Central government intervenes to dictate certain responsibilities and prefers accountability to itself rather than to the local recipients of those services. Jobs therefore have to be constructed from a mixed set of responsibilities that are in part internal and in part external to the organization.

On a general point, we should be readier to accept the proposition that human society may be better served by local decisions made by local teams, where humans can operate in the size groupings for which they have been designed by evolution. The caveat is that these teams must be as carefully chosen as in sport. Effective teams, of limited size, need to contain the best players (in insect terms the appropriate caste members). The ability to compose a well-balanced team is the prime caste skill of the manager. If society is to be re-invented, we need also to re-invent the role of the people manager, who now in this technological age has the scope to handle a far wider database than at any period in history. Such a manager should not be conceived as a wielder of power outside his or her caste skill, nor be esteemed more highly than other key players. These, as people professionals, can make valuable contributions in their own special way. But those skills will have even more radical consequences when they can be passed on to the teams themselves. The benefit would be that team members would be able to revitalize and renew the vigour of their own teams. That is exactly what the social insects do. They are not *people managed* by others; they respond to the sensory cues they receive from other insects and they adjust their behaviours. Mutualism and lateral accountability are the concepts closest to the way in which they respond to the changing threats and opportunities that their environment poses.

Lateral accountability is largely suppressed by procedures favoured in large bureaucracies. The old hierarchical system of salary determination according to individual performance, as judged from above, becomes an impediment to pulling together and reinforces the separation of authority levels. People are often locked into jobs because it becomes too politically complicated to extend their frontiers or to widen experience by moving between jobs. So wherever they are, they stay, while their organizations become increasingly obsolete in terms of what they deliver.

A map of work roles, now technically possible, helps one to understand the general pattern of how large organizations actually function. However organizations project their cultural image, the common reality is usually very different, or at least confused. Still, hierarchies generally prevail. In the private sector, one boss has the power to overrule another and, as one proceeds down the power hierarchy, there is a change in the colour spectrum as pure Yellow gives way to pure Blue. In the public sector, the colour spectrum takes on a different hue. Green and Blue work abound, the former taking the form of discussions and the latter as regulations. Yellow and Orange work seldom exist in their most desired forms, for decision-making is constrained by the concept of 'checks and balances'. Decisions are referred or recommended to some other level in a hierarchy or between officials and elected members. They move to and fro in a complex process that resists intervention. Decision-making is further delayed and undermined by appeal systems. In the supposed interests of justice, legal appeals in some countries can take over a decade while the appellant remains on Death Row. Generally, appeals disempower decision-makers, presume that better deci-sions are made elsewhere and introduce huge delays, in the planning and construction fields especially, that critically affect socially important projects.

Can human mega-groups become supergroups? That is the big question. Clearly the answer is *Yes* in isolated cases but one doubts whether a more general transformation can be made without a radical change in the social outlook. As a species, humans must recognize they have faults that cannot be counted as *allowable weaknesses*. They should be humble enough to realize that they can learn from other creatures. That is why in Chapter 13 I have given such attention to the *superorganism*. That may remain a model beyond our immediate reach. But appreciating it may help us to reappraise the way we work and move towards the half-way stage of the supergroup.

To recap what has been said, the true superorganism lacks a command and control system based on single-person power. In the case of the social insects it functions instead through the integrated deployment of information freely circulating through a colony of mobile workers with specialist skills. The way in which that information is used enables the right specialist skills to be present in the areas where they can be used to best effect in the interests of the colony as a whole. That does not mean that all social insects have an equally important role to play. There are times when one insect has an overwhelmingly important influence on decision-making. Take the case of a single scout wasp discovering an excellent site for a new nest and conveying this to a large wasp colony by means of an excited dance. That wasp in effect determines the relocation of the colony. A site for relocation may also be a critical issue for a large human organization. The decision will not be taken on the basis of a popularity poll but be taken by a single person or even better by a small strategic team. In this sense humans are no more elitist than insects. Particular insects are empowered to do particular things. The more important distinction is that the decision-making power of the scout wasp is not generalized. It is only in a particular context that the scout wasp has such a big role to play. Herein lies the difference between the politics of the world of the social insects and that of humans. Humans broaden and perpetuate their power once it is secured. The social insects do not.

Using feedback in a co-ordinated way to enlarge our understanding of what individuals can bring to a job (their team roles) and how they actually perform (their work roles) has only become feasible recently. That step, rendered possible by advancing technology, means that people, like insects, can use their senses to input and transmit information for a common purpose. Computers can now store, sift and retrieve detailed people-information and advise on how they may be best deployed. The technological revolution promises at least to make us as well equipped in sensory resources as the social insects. The super-organism therefore acts as a model from which much can be learned. For genetic reasons, the superorganism in its purest form remains largely beyond human reach. But what is attainable for the mega-group is to move in the direction of the superorganism by endeavouring to become a supergroup in ways that remain characteristically human.

So what are the lessons that can be learned? The ideal field of application might seem to lie in the public sector with its lack of an obvious command and control structure, where power is spread between permanent officials and elected representatives. It is the model of democracy to which we have grown accustomed. Yet its shortcoming is that it has neither the functional clarity of the solo-led group nor the mutually supportive and co-operative nature of the supergroup. The competitive elective nature of democracy, which is group- rather than person-based, fosters confrontational relationships. Here, it may be contended, the best prospect for public sector bodies is to move in the direction of supergroups by creating and nurturing multi-stage local empowerment. For local empowerment to succeed in a work form, it must be free from the risk of disempowerment by an all-powerful central body and equally from the risk of creating local fiefdoms, which in effect can only lead to fragmenting the coherence of the supergroup. A holistic system can only maintain its stability through interacting subsystems that combine to strengthen the whole. So locally selected and *known* individuals need to move between groups lest the work of the subgroup should only serve its own interests. This lateral career movement will become most effective where groups can be reconstructed as teams and teams improved by transfer in and transfer out of suitable members.

If one asks how far this is happening to any significant extent in either public or private sector organizations, the answer must be *very little*. Humans are not genetically predisposed to being built into superorganisms. The journey in this direction will be difficult and slow. But there is a positive side. Modification of normal modes of functioning in large groups remains a possibil-ity. Humans do alter *natural* behaviour in a desired direction through education and training. A sophisticated society has the capacity to project and facilitate models of behaviour that lie beyond historical precedent. There is mounting pressure to move

away from patterns of behaviour that have been known to fail in the past. The targets are cumbersome public bureaucracies and industrial conglomerates that fail to reach their potential. The climate of the times favours change. Even *thriving on chaos* is seen as a better alternative to bureaucratic stagnation. The forms of human organization that have predominated in the past and at one time played a significant part in the evolution of human society have now lost their competitive advantage. Many high tech companies, employing very talented individuals, secure their services in employment by freeing them from the controls that would be seen as normal in outsize organizations.

How will this type of flexible approach work out in practice? Career development and the rotation of individuals through jobs allow the skills of individuals to emerge and be identified by close colleagues. The information can be computer-stored and easily retrieved, not so much by Big Brother as typically feared, as by teams keen to improve their performance. In public affairs there is the prospect that local government would thrive, whereas at present it lies emasculated under the weight of central government. Local elections have low turnouts. Significantly, the swing generally depends more on the image of the leader of central government than on the competence of local representatives. People consider they know more about national figures than they do about those in their own neighbourhood. And it is almost certainly true that they do. The devolution of responsibility is the means whereby relationships in local government, and with the public at large, could be radically changed.

Which should come first? Should we set out to change the way jobs are set up or to change the nature of organization? I have little doubt myself which is the more favourable route. The larger the group, the more conservative its procedures become. But the way jobs are set up lies open to change: the way teams are fostered instead of groups; the way large is cut down to small where all meetings are concerned. There is a lot that can readily be done now. It is this pattern of progressive change in work roles that lays the foundation for an eventual transformation in organizational shape.

16

Snakes and ladders

Improving communications about the job opens up the road to progress with benefits available for both the private and public sectors of the economy. The language of work roles is intricate and precise: jobholders understand more about what is expected from them and managers understand more about what is actually going on. Yet the gains are not confined to better communication. The rapid interflow of information has not only enabled jobs to deliver more but has provided general lessons on the best ways of organizing work.

Finding a better way of approaching *the job* should lead on to an improved outflow in the efficiency of organization. Yet that strategy still faces unwelcome hazards, for experience shows that in the complex fabric of human society nothing that is started remains within its chosen limits. Every innovation has some impact on the ecosystem in which it is encased. Either the ecosystem changes to accommodate the innovation or the stability of the original system re-establishes itself in its totality by rejecting what cannot be assimilated.

There is therefore a choice. Should one start by grasping the new paradigm, by linking the concept of partnership in the setting up and development of jobs with a different approach to career development, to the appraisal of people, to job enlargement and to reward systems? Or is it preferable to start with a very modest objective at the local level and to accept at least for the time being the *status quo*? The choice of the former would be ideal. The reality is that large change is seldom feasible within a limited time frame. The only positive alternative is to take small steps forward in a given direction, which means facing up to the consequences of a possible backlash as change takes root.

The latter strategy, modest though it may be in its objective, will still have to contend with obstacles and opposition. Consider now the position with the centrepiece of this book – the system used to clarify communication between parties with a common interest in jobs. Colour-based work roles have special application in bridging the gap between people who lack a common first language or whose oral styles of communication are barriers to understanding. That language has enabled futile work to be highlighted and so removed and has given a boost to improving what can be improved. Top-down communication has been replaced with a circulating communication system, which is more sensitive to the needs of situations. Adding value to the job generates a lot of pluses, which taken together resemble a ladder. This ladder to progress offers a sure way of getting better results from limited resources. That is the good news. But now for the bad news. It seems that whenever the ladder of progress is erected, there, unseen in the long grass, lies a snake – an echo of the well-known board game of snakes and ladders. While it is important to climb a ladder, it is equally important to avoid the snakes (see Figure 11).

It is difficult to imagine there might be a problem here. Yet it is easy to be mistaken, for as one person produces more, the effect can be that an equivalent quantity of work is extracted from the actual or potential duties of others. So the overall output remains the same in a zero-sum game. People take the line: 'Well, if one person is doing all the work and doing it well, we can relax.' That is the snake. It is not obvious and people seldom look for it. This lurking danger means that for every step mounted, another is liable to result in rapid descent to the foot of the ladder. Beyond a small circle no one may be aware that gains were made, even if only temporarily, in some limited area of the business.

There is, however, a clear solution to this problem. If the gains registered are to be consolidated, a further step has to be taken. The view must prevail that no job exists in isolation. Adjacent jobs have to be tackled as a *group* to ensure that gains occur in the *overall* output of goods or services. This holistic approach is incorporated in *process re-engineering*, now an acknowledged means of adding value to jobs. Such opportunities exist because jobs have a way of continuing unchanged in a changing world, moving steadily towards obsolescence, until someone does something about them. Even so, much process re-engineering disappoints. Experience shows that this ladder to progress is itself subject to a hazard from a snake. People are disinclined to have their jobs tampered with; they jealously guard what is familiar; they protect themselves from what they see as intrusion into their familiar job territory. Happily, there is here too a ready solution. Process re-engineering seldom works well without taking into account the team roles of those being redeployed and of their intended work associates. An extra dimension to the effectiveness of redeployment has been added by the concept of work roles, so ensuring that the work of individuals and teams matches the changing demands of the external world. Once again, if upward steps are to be taken on the ladder, team roles and work roles need to be taken together. However, this is a complex process, demanding much nurturing if the process is to bring about the desired results.

We have now climbed two rungs up the ladder of added value. But keeping that foothold is still not guaranteed. One further step needs to be taken if success is to be consolidated. The mature team needs *empowerment*. That notion has been widely canvassed and supported. Yet, as so often happens with favoured themes, it has faded from view almost as quickly as it came into the spotlight of publicity. The snake that lurks at this higher level is not inertia: it is the reluctance of management to empower. A mature team cannot empower itself. The empowering agent must be management, which itself has to submit to a form of disempowerment if it is to empower others. That significant impediment is even harder to overcome when management has invested in those top-down personnel methodologies generally favoured by hierarchies. No top manager who has recommended the financial outlay that such an investment requires in conventional HR policies is likely to retract from what is already established. Such a retraction would be tantamount to an admission: 'I have wasted the firm's money.' So a large snake lies in waiting to devour the climber.

Suppose we lull this snake to sleep and now stand, secure for the moment, high on the ladder. The mature team is flourishing and comprises mature people. Such people require, and have the right to expect, career development. But career development does not sit happily alongside formal job evaluation. If one moves the person from job to job in the interests of gaining experience, a complication ensues. How is that person to be paid? Does that person carry a personal level of remuneration irrespective of the job being done? Or are people to be paid according to the job they do? In the latter case earnings would fluctuate as people moved from job to job. In the case of a supposedly less demanding job, there would be a loss of earnings. The fostering of career development along with a policy of encouraging job flexibility together disrupt the tidy administration of pay based on evaluation of the job. The protectors of job evaluation are alerted and the snake is aroused from its slumbers.

Effective empowerment of people, if all the hurdles are overcome, enables several upward steps to be taken on the ladder. A high point has been reached but the foothold is insecure. Teams and groups are intermingling, as success swells the numbers brought into the enterprise. Once the group turns into a mega-group, the greater is the likelihood that the team will be swallowed up and that it will be difficult for empowerment to survive. But it is not impossible. A teamworking culture, valuing team spirit, can be fostered by a wise manager. People will take on both team and group identities. They will be imbued with the *esprit de corps* that characterizes groups that are well led. And they will bask in the sense of personal identity that a team culture allows. In such a scenario the large group will not lose its capacity for strategic direction, because teamwork is embodied in its strategic leadership. Such a *mega-group* is on its way to becoming a *supergroup*. Such a transformation is unlikely to take place without the presence of a person with the appropriate qualities and skills at its head. In the supergroup the leader does not dominate decisions but controls the process. Such forbearance demands strong character attributes. Happily, such managers are to be found, even though they are scarce. That is why the educational development of managers is of such importance.

104

We have now climbed high up the ladder of added value. *Controlled empowerment* will have taken root. Whenever that position has been reached, people have conspicuously delivered more from their jobs. Yet too much is easily taken for granted. Consolidation cannot be assumed. The supergroup has no guaranteed permanence because its licence to continue depends on its leadership. A death, a retirement or an overthrow means that everything may change. Where the concept of the supergroup can justifiably be applied to nations it will depend on its constitution. Small nations may continue to exercise some of the characteristics of the supergroup but large nations are liable to be pulled back by the limitations attached to any size colossus. The supergroup is prone to revert to the mega-group from which it sprang. Meetings will embrace groups and not teams. And humans will be called to participate in size groupings for which they are unfitted.

As groups get larger, the sense of anonymity that membership of large groups brings in its wake creates the need for a hero or saviour personality, capable of conveying a sense of intimacy with the group. Yet far from being a personal relationship, the relationship becomes more distant. The new Mr Big will be keen to be bigger, and seen to be bigger, than other managers. I have argued that the psychological roots of that difficulty – the supersnake that affects the whole of mankind – are genetic and therefore widespread. Teams soon begin to be undone, in their powers at least. The new Mr Big says, in effect, 'I am the boss; I will decide.' Such a person would hardly declare, 'I believe you are better placed to decide. So I am transferring that responsibility to you.'

As groups get larger, the pressures for the arrival of a solo leader increase. Dynasties or the possible overthrow of dynasties preoccupy the attention of people and dominate their conduct of affairs. Solo leadership prevails. Kings, Emperors, Presidents or Chief Executives, following one another in due line of succession, have throughout history been disposed to place an individual stamp on their period of rule. So in almost random fashion the benign has been followed by the wicked, centralists by devolutionists, hands-on leaders by those who have been happy to opt out and leave responsibility to lieutenants. There is no way of knowing what succession may bring in its wake. A new Mr Big may cancel all that has been achieved at a stroke by adopting a style incompatible with all that has gone before. Great civilizations or industrial corporations may be undermined in a fraction of the time taken to build them.

Is there a solution to the problems of managing the mega-group, which in spite of the efforts of image-makers is too large to allow for effective personal control? How can achievements be stabilized in an unstable world? The lesson from nature is that perhaps the best prospect for the mega-group is to transform itself into the holistic robustness of the supergroup. Just as in teams, diversity in abilities and personal attributes adds strength, so also in supergroups the checks and balances of the body corporate ensure its continuity and health. Supergroups are bound together by functions and institutions that operate coherently together and by abstract notions that promote unity and a sense of some common ideal, tradition or historical experience.

A nation can provide a good model of a supergroup: it is too large for its members ever to assemble at one spot; it may comprise people of different ethnic groups, languages and religions. Yet its institutions operate as a holistic entity that is not susceptible to the whims or fancies of a ruler. Such an example is Switzerland. (There is a saying 'Does anyone know the name of the Swiss Prime Minister?' This can be said jeeringly. But I see it as a compliment.) Divided by three principal languages plus one minor language, Switzerland embraces two principal and historically antagonistic religions and the usual medley of political parties. Yet it still retains its essentially Swiss character and its famed stability. Switzerland has the smallest share of the national income taken by any central government and the lowest degree of centralization of functions of any world country. Devolved powers add strength because wider use can be made of the skills and abilities latent in smaller groups and teams. The small can inspire the large.

Ultimately the health of the whole, whether a nation or a corporation, depends on the vitality of its parts. For the parts to flourish a common understanding is needed on what constitutes duty and responsibility. People need to know what is expected from them. They need a common language to talk about both personal and corporate relationships. And if they lack a common mother tongue, they need a technical language to create unambiguous meaning.

People at work, whether in business or in the private sector, will not reach the maturity that a growing world requires until they are able to combine a global vision with the freedom to act locally. That combination requires a particular set of conditions. Where these can be created, people will be better placed to amend what they see as failing in their own working environments. The sum of their efforts will then become a major force for community advancement.

Balanced teamwork and the equitable distribution of responsibilities, based on a careful analysis of needs, are important at every level. In this sense team roles and work roles have a universality of application. Advances may only occur in faltering steps, for every level involves different types of political complexity and hazard. Yet there is an underlying similarity in the problems that do occur and they largely centre on communication and a sense of common purpose. It is hoped that the language system introduced in this book, together with the philosophy that forms its foundation, may find a general application.

In the past hundred years humans have climbed from a low point in the conduct of work organization and public affairs to a middle position on the ladder of progress. We now look upwards in expectation and downwards in dread. Can we climb further upwards without falling back again? Will we become prey to a supersnake that is forever waiting? We do not know. The likelihood is that we will continue to play snakes and ladders. This situation will prevail until human evolution moves in the direction of the superorganism. Only then can the sum total of individual talents operate for the common good.

1

The language of work roles

Illustrations of how precise meanings can be conveyed orally

Examples of how managers can bring about the required approach to a job

BLUE
Remember what you've been taught Make sure that it's working correctly Come and see me again if you're in any doubt Check that it's in line with the specification

YELLOW
You will be judged by results It's your responsibility to decide You will have to take a view, one way or another If you can find another solution, so much the better

GREEN
Make sure that the customer (client, patient) feels happy Remember it's not what you do but how you do it that matters Don't keep customers (clients, patients) waiting See what you can do to help

ORANGE
It is essential that you all agree Don't push for a decision if you feel there are lingering doubts Remember that you are sharing responsibility Make sure you are playing the right support role in the team

Examples of use by jobholders in reporting on work outside the core roles

GREY
I was short of materials, so I went to collect some
During the waiting time, I tidied up the office
I've been giving a helping hand to reduce the backlog
I've spent some time covering for X's absence

PINK
I've been called to a meeting for a reason that's not clear to me
None of this information I've been collecting appears to be used
I've been sorting out stock I know to be obsolete
Most of the data I've been compiling is out-of-date

WHITE
I've been reorganizing the files
I thought I would create my own register
I've found a good way of making contact with a potential customer
As it was not working properly, I got it repaired

2

Glossary with added notes

Individuals: key people

Team player
A person who can manage the role of the self to fit the needs of a team. Well-qualified applicants who lack this quality are often rejected for appointment.

Manager
The core work of a manager may be defined as assigning tasks, responsibilities and contracts to others. While managers undertake a host of miscellaneous activities, the core work of a manager relates to those activities which are *uniquely* managerial. Other managerial activities such as planning, financial control and communication may be shared with consultants, professionals and non-executive directors. A person who is accomplished in the core work is likely to be recognized as a *good manager*, even if deficient in a wide range of other accomplishments.

Worker
One who is only given tasks by a manager. Unskilled and most semi-skilled work is performed by workers.

Jobholder
One whose duties at work comprise both tasks and responsibilities. Most newly created jobs are set up for jobholders rather than workers.

Roles

Team role
The tendency to behave, contribute and interrelate with others in a particular way. A team role signifies the contributions someone is typically disposed to make in interpersonal working relationships. The hyphenated term indicates its adjectival use, as in *team-role profile*, and is employed to remove any possible ambiguities of meaning.

Functional role
A functional role refers to how a person is expected to perform on the basis of the job title and supposed duties. Often those presumptions are misplaced.

Professional role
The professional role refers to the qualifications and formal training that a person brings to the job. Professionals often find it difficult to see the distinction between their role and the nature of the job.

Work role
A work role relates to the tasks and responsibilities undertaken by individuals or executed within teams. There are four core categories of work used by managers to assign work – Blue, Yellow, Green and Orange – and three additional categories used by the jobholder to report additional work undertaken – Grey, White and Pink (see below).

Role-fulfilment
This term relates to the gratification that comes to the self from finding an appropriate role in a team. Offering an appropriate role opportunity constitutes one of the most simple and effective ways of motivating individuals.

Work assigned by the manager

Task
A task is an item of work that has to be performed in accordance with instructions. Tasks comprise the following:

Blue work
Blue work covers prescribed tasks that need to be performed by a particular person to a particular standard. Blue work is commonly demanded where considerations of health, safety and efficiency are given due priority.

Green work
Green work refers to tasks that may be performed in a non-standard way according to the circumstances in which the work is carried out. Green work predominates wherever there is a prime need for responsiveness to patients, clients or customers.

Responsibility
A responsibility relates to a goal or objective for which a person (singly) or persons (jointly) are held accountable. Responsibilities fall into two categories:

Yellow work
Yellow work refers to a responsibility assigned to an individual and which allows full personal discretion.

Orange work
Orange work refers to work where responsibility and decision-making need to be shared by several people, as in a team.

In medium-sized and large firms most managers will have some Yellow work and some Orange work. However, they often have difficulty in knowing which applies where.

Additional work discovered by the jobholder

Grey work
Grey work occurs when the jobholder expands the core work of the job by incorporating activities perceived as making a useful contribution. Grey work may not be required but is usually appreciated when it occurs.

White work
White work embodies new activities outside the range of the core work and not expected by the manager to whom the jobholder is responsible. White work will, however, need to be reported in order to ascertain that the initiative is acceptable.

Pink work
Pink work arises where the jobholder is engaged in a work activity which he or she believes to be valueless but from which there is no escape.

Organization

Group
A group refers to a number of people brought together for a common purpose while being too numerous to allow team-role relationships to from. As numbers in the group increase, the identity and special role contribution of every individual member diminishes and correspondingly the role of the leader becomes enlarged.

Team
A team comprises a limited number of people selected to work together for a shared objective in a way that allows each person to make a distinctive contribution. A well-balanced team will encompass all the team roles required for an effective perform-ance, but should not be so large that team roles are duplicated and liable to produce dysfunctional role competition. While the size of the team will depend on the situation, a favoured size is four. With proper selection that number should enable most desired team roles to be adequately covered and will also enable rotating leadership to develop.

Mature team
A team becomes mature when its understanding of the strengths and limitations of its individual players is combined with an awareness of external needs. The team is then well placed to distribute work among its own members without the inter-vention of a manager.

Mega-group
A mega-group describes a group too large for the person in charge to become personally known or even casually acquainted

with more than a small minority. A mega-group will find it hard to operate as a cohesive and like-minded body of people under the supervision of a single personality without evolving into a multi-layered hierarchy, served by a controlling bureaucracy.

Supergroup
A supergroup will grow out of a mega-group through an organizational transformation, when particular responsibilities are passed on to institutions or corporate bodies rather than to individuals. The agent for assigning work then becomes the institution or the corporate body. However, the supergroup is prone to become fragmented once the parts take on an independent life of their own.

Superorganism
The superorganism represents a higher stage of organization than the supergroup. The character of the whole body retains its basic stability through an intricate decentralized system involving the autonomous yet co-operative interaction of its parts. Superorganisms make free use of specialists. The leadership function within the human superorganism can be undertaken by a team strong in strategic and co-ordination skills.

Groupthink
The watershed concept separating teams and groups. The concept of groupthink was first created by Irving Janis (*Groupthink: Psychological Studies of Policy Decisions and Fiascos*, Houghton Mifflin, New York, 1982). Groupthink has been described as a 'mode of thinking that people engage in when deeply involved in a cohesive in-group and when the striving for unanimity overrides the motivation to realistically appraise alternative courses of action'. Groupthink, it is claimed, can cause a smart bunch of people to come up with a very incompetent solution. That tendency is amplified as the size of group increases.

Continued study of groupthink has led to a modified definition within this book and now refers simply to the phenomenon whereby 'a group of people too large to form a team are prone to think alike and to follow the same illusions'. So large groups rapidly become inefficient unless they can be restructured into interacting, well composed, empowered and dynamic teams.

Index

Waiting time, as Pink work, 29–30
Watson, Barrie, 64
White work, 58
 definition, 24–5, 114
 examples, 110
Work activities, colour allocation,
 23–5
Work distribution, alternatives, 41
Work group, 13
 autonomous, 20
 and team distinction, 14, 17
Work organization, superorganism
 model, 80
Work roles:
 definition, 19, 112
 effect on payment systems, *see*
  Payment systems

mapping, 97
pioneer systems, 78
proactive use of language, 72
trial colour systems, 62, 71–2, 102,
 108–10
Work-culture, 40–1
Worker, definition, 111

Yellow work, 49, 53, 70, 109
 definition, 23, 113
 payment systems, 47, 48
 redistribution from solo leader,
  90–1
 and solo leader role, 88
 transfer, 77

Team Roles at Work

R. Meredith Belbin, *Belbin Associates*

This book, a follow-up to the best-selling **Management Teams: Why They Succeed or Fail**, develops Belbin's ideas using feedback gained from the users of his work.

The nine team roles, now familiar to managers and management trainers all over the world, are explored further, adding value to the original team-role concepts. Operational strategies are laid out which provide ideas, techniques and a new range of information and advice which can be used to the organization's advantage.

Team Roles at Work paves the way for all those in management education, including industrial trainers to put Belbin's seminal thinking on teams into practice.

ISBN 0 7506 2675 5, 160pp, 234 x 156mm, paperback, 1996, £16.99

HOW TO ORDER
Heinemann Customer Services, Halley Court, Jordan Hill, Oxford OX2 8EJ
Tel: 01865 888180   Fax: 01865 314290   http://www.bh.com